Innocence Unveiled

Michele Ruyters • Gregory Stratton
Alyssa Sigamoney • Monique Moffa
Jarryd Bartle

Innocence Unveiled

The Systemic, Social, and Structural Factors Behind Wrongful Convictions in Australia

palgrave
macmillan

Michele Ruyters
School of Global, Urban, Social Studies
RMIT University
Melbourne, VIC, Australia

Gregory Stratton
School of Global, Urban, Social Studies
RMIT University
Melbourne, VIC, Australia

Alyssa Sigamoney
School of Global, Urban, Social Studies
RMIT University
Melbourne, VIC, Australia

Monique Moffa
School of Global, Urban, Social Studies
RMIT University
Melbourne, VIC, Australia

Jarryd Bartle
School of Global, Urban, Social Studies
RMIT University
Melbourne, VIC, Australia

ISBN 978-3-031-91342-6 ISBN 978-3-031-91343-3 (eBook)
https://doi.org/10.1007/978-3-031-91343-3

This Palgrave Macmillan imprint is published by the registered company Springer Nature Switzerland AG.
The registered company address is: Gewerbestrasse 11, 6330 Cham, Switzerland

If disposing of this product, please recycle the paper.

Competing Interests

The authors have no competing interests to declare that are relevant to the content of this manuscript.

Contents

About the Authors

Jarryd Bartle is Lecturer in Criminology and Justice Studies at RMIT University and a consultant for the Bridge of Hope Innocence Initiative, which investigates claims of wrongful conviction and advocates for systemic reform to protect against miscarriages of justice.

Monique Moffa is Lecturer in Criminology and Justice Studies at RMIT University and a supervisor at RMIT's Bridge of Hope Innocence Initiative. Monique's research interests focus on wrongful conviction, parole, and the reintegration of individuals who have experienced a miscarriage of justice. Monique is also a PhD student at Monash University, focusing on defendant experiences of plea negotiations.

Michele Ruyters is Professor and Associate Dean of Criminology and Justice Studies at RMIT University. She is the founder and director of the Bridge of Hope Innocence Initiative and the Bridge of Hope Criminal Case Review Project at RMIT University and leads all case investigations. Professor Ruyters' practice and research interests are in wrongful conviction and miscarriages of justice, with a focus on police non-disclosure and accountability, post-conviction review, and the causes of wrongful convictions.

Alyssa Sigamoney is Lecturer in Criminology and Justice Studies at RMIT University and a supervisor at RMIT's Bridge of Hope Innocence Initiative. Alyssa's practice and research areas include the role of racism in wrongful convictions as well as miscarriages of justice and post-conviction review processes more broadly. Alyssa is completing a PhD at Monash Law, researching defendants experiences of post-conviction review processes in Australia.

Gregory Stratton is Senior Lecturer in Justice and Legal Studies at RMIT University and is also the co-founder and manager of the Bridge of Hope Innocence Initiative at RMIT University. His research interests focus on wrongful conviction, state crime, media and crime, and digital criminology. He has published regularly on wrongful conviction with the book *Streaming Justice—True Crime and Wrongful Conviction in the Streaming Age* (Springer), due for publication in 2025. He has previously co-authored the book *Digital Criminology: Crime and Justice in Digital Society* (Routledge, 2018).

CHAPTER 1

Introduction

Abstract This chapter introduces a perspective on wrongful conviction rooted in practical experience with the Bridge of Hope Innocence Initiative at RMIT University. Working within an Australian context where DNA exonerations are rare, the chapter begins with a call for a broader understanding of wrongful conviction beyond a singular focus on particular causes or even formal exoneration. By introducing the tragedy of wrongful convictions and emphasising the global movement advocating for the innocent, the chapter highlights how the US successes have spurred international interest but have had limited success in assisting the innocent outside the US. Drawing on our Australian experience, we reveal how case, systemic, and cultural complexities have limited success in Australia. While acknowledging the groundwork of our international peers, we critique the Australian and international reliance on US-centric, DNA-focused exonerations and causal factor analyses, arguing for a broader understanding of wrongful convictions by examining risks, systemic failures, and socio-cultural influences. Through the lens of wrongful conviction practitioners, the chapter advocates for moving beyond defining innocence solely through exonerations to include a wider array of experiences and claims to foster more effective research, advocacy, and reform.

Keywords Wrongful conviction • Risk • Causal factors • Systemic issues • Innocence

M. Ruyters et al., *Innocence Unveiled*,
https://doi.org/10.1007/978-3-031-91343-3_1

Wrongful convictions are an all-too-common tragedy. The suffering endured by the innocent when punished for crimes they did not commit demands a deep reflection on the operation of the criminal justice system and a critique of those who contributed to errors leading to injustice. Within legal and academic circles, these reflections often prompt a search for answers, seeking to understand why the criminal justice system has failed. However, like most social phenomena, we rarely identify a singular reason for why the fault occurred, nor does a singular solution exist to improve the experience of those who are wrongfully convicted and punished.

Despite the complexity of the problem, a growing number of academics, legal professionals, and advocates continue to build a global movement raising awareness about wrongful convictions. This support is expansive, on display in courtrooms, parliaments, universities, the media, and anywhere a voice to advocate for the innocent is required. The tireless work of innocence advocates has made significant progress towards understanding how systems fail and in stimulating public awareness of the problem of wrongful convictions (Dwyer et al., 2001). A catalyst to this understanding has been the prevalence of DNA-based exonerations in the United States, which enabled advocates to centre on specific case errors with irrefutable proof of error (Medwed, 2017; Innocence Project, 2023). Led by the work of the Innocence Project established in 1992 by Peter Neufeld and Barry Scheck, the project provided a platform for advocates to free the innocent, prevent wrongful convictions, and create fair, compassionate, and equitable systems of justice for everyone (Dwyer et al., 2001; Innocence Project, 2024a). From their first DNA exoneration of Glenn Woodall in 1992 to the time of writing in 2024, the Innocence Project has exonerated over 250 people, more than 200 of them using DNA to prove innocence and help solve crimes (Innocence Project, 2024b). Many similar projects emerged in the ensuing years, recognising the scope of injustice experienced by the wrongfully convicted around the United States (for a history of this movement, see Norris, 2017). Variations in the project mimicked the focus on DNA, while others expanded their approach to explore other forms of exculpatory evidence. With over 50 innocence projects in the US over the past 30 years (Innocence Network, 2024a), more than 3600 people have been exonerated (National Registry of Exonerations, 2024).

The success of innocence work in the US in exonerating the innocent and contributing to significant justice system reform spurred an extended innocence network that has seen the evolution of innocence projects worldwide, including Australia (Godsey, 2017; Robins, 2023; Le et al., 2023). Primed by the DNA-led exoneration success in the US, the international experience of wrongful conviction, exoneration, and innocence-based advocacy has, however, been less straightforward. For international projects, the American experience has provided global momentum and rationale for focusing resources towards fighting for the innocent (Godsey, 2017).

The success of these US exonerations has seen significant global academic interest, policy focus, and reform in specific areas of failure (Gould & Leo, 2010; Garrett, 2020; Norris et al., 2021). For those of us working in this space, these points of failure are very familiar points of critique. Recognising fundamental failings in police investigations, prosecutorial decision-making, forensic errors, eyewitness testimony, and other biases within the criminal justice system have become hallmarks of our advocacy and sites of reform and change. However, crucially for those outside of the US, the experience of advocating for the wrongfully convicted and understanding how it occurs has differed significantly from our American peers. This book is about the Australian context of wrongful conviction and reflects the experiences and learnings of an Australian innocence project, the Bridge of Hope Innocence Initiative.

Wrongful Conviction Advocacy in Australia

While today the US advocacy model of wrongful conviction approaches miscarriages of justice through many avenues, DNA evidence was seen as an important catalyst for exonerations because it offers a certain conclusivity that enables policy reform and public support. In comparison, Australian experiences of wrongful conviction with advocacy highlight additional complexities. Notably, few Australian wrongful convictions over the past 30 years have been unveiled through DNA evidence (Blewer et al., 2023). In the absence of DNA's conclusivity, the examination of wrongful conviction in Australia has tended to involve scrutiny of a broader range of factors and influences as a means of seeking justice. From Andrew Mallard to Gene Gibson to Kathleen Folbigg, Australian wrongful convictions have not relied upon the irrefutable proof of DNA. Instead, their successful exonerations expose a multifaceted layer of issues related to wrongful conviction rather than single solutions.

Consider, for example, the complexities involved in the wrongful conviction and eventual government pardon of Kathleen Folbigg in 2023 after she spent 20 years in prison for the deaths of her four infant children (*Folbigg v The King* [2023] NSWCCA 325). A 2022 inquiry into her conviction heard evidence from medical experts that highlighted genetic factors as the cause of death. A petition led by immunologist Professor Carola Gacia de Vinuesa and signed by over 100 scientists was an essential factor in demonstrating that two of the children had genetic mutations that predisposed them to heart complications (de Vinuesa, 2021). These claims were based on new scientific understandings of *CALM* gene mutations that presented a 'reasonable explanation for a natural cause' of death in two of Folbigg's children (Brohus et al., 2021). This knowledge was unavailable when Folbigg was convicted in 2003. At trial, the prosecution relied upon problematic, gendered interpretations of Folbigg's diaries (Cunliffe, 2011) and problematic epidemiological interpretations about the rarity of one family experiencing multiple cases of Sudden Infant Death Syndrome (SIDS) that had not been discredited at the time of Folbigg's trial (Bathurst, 2022, p. 81). This new scientific endeavour was able to call into question the initial evidence and lead to her pardon.

For 20 years, despite appeals, inquiries, and an application for judicial review, Folbigg had no viable opportunity to overturn her conviction until new medical advancements emerged. However, even before the recent genetic evidence, her case had already contained credible circumstantial, medical, and pathology evidence indicating her children had died of natural causes (de Vinuesa, 2021). Her case also demonstrated issues in the police investigation and prosecution, suggesting gendered bias and assumptions that have been demonstrated in other high-profile wrongful convictions of women and mothers (Cunliffe, 2011). For this reason, it would be too simplistic to explain that Folbigg's wrongful conviction was overturned simply because we now have access to better science. Nor was the medical evidence and pathology diagnosis the sole factor behind her conviction.

Much like the momentum of DNA-led exonerations overseas in the early 2000s, the success of Folbigg's case created a new impetus for the innocence movement in Australia. It has led to calls for a focus on the significant problems in forensic and medical science presented in some Australian cases (Cordner & Breen, 2023). There are also calls for the establishment of an independent body like the United Kingdom's Criminal Case Review Commission (CCRC) to provide a systemic solution for the systemic risk of wrongful conviction (Hamer & Dwyer, 2023; Cordner &

Breen, 2023; but see Ruyters & Bartle, 2024). While these approaches have merit, and any reform assisting the wrongfully convicted should be considered, they focus on past events with the benefit of hindsight and provide little evidence that reforms such as these address the actual needs of the currently incarcerated innocent. While systemic options like CCRCs or the conviction integrity units that are established in the United States may reduce the threshold for challenging errors, they have a limited capacity to identify underlying factors leading to those errors. Suggestions that individual scientific advances will lead to a robust systemic effort to address Australia's wrongful convictions are shortsighted because they overlook where injustice occurs, how injustice happens, and who experiences injustice. For cases that rest on science, it may be too difficult to progress to a claim of wrongful conviction without available advances to reinterpret the evidence presented in the trial.

Scientific and medical evidence is crucial in developing a better understanding of wrongful conviction but must be considered alongside a range of factors within Australia's multi-tiered criminal justice system, which both contribute to and offer solutions for errors in the system. A common perception of criminal justice is as singular branches, such as policing, courts, and corrections that operate with independence and objectivity. The reality is that the branches overlap with a range of social, cultural, political, scientific, and economic paradigms that influence their decision-making and effectiveness in addressing crime and justice issues. Despite allusions of transparency and rigour to suggest the contrary, these elements are susceptible to human failing, systemic failure, structural barriers, and societal bias, which can lead to error. Even if only one element is initially at fault, their intersections and operations often bring the others to fault. For this reason, even when science might provide answers, there is an emphasis on comprehensive reform instead of specific areas of need. The complexity and diversity of issues involved in identifying wrongful convictions have prompted Australian innocence advocates to move beyond a binary approach and recognise the interconnectedness and overlapping of contributing factors.

Our approach is focused on recognising these intersections and identifying the wide range of risks that contribute to an environment in which wrongful convictions can occur in Australia and potentially globally. While the range is broad, our aim is to identify specific risks to ensure the experiences of the wrongfully convicted are not overgeneralised or ambiguously categorised. Knowledge and understanding of what contributes to wrongful conviction have expanded in recent times but have been slow or reticent to expand beyond Borchardian categorisation, which has dominated our understanding of why the innocent suffer.

Borchardian Categorisation and the Limits of Causal Factors

Edwin Borchard's seminal *Convicting the Innocent* (1932) stands as one of the most significant explorations of wrongful conviction. It marks the beginning of nearly a century's reflection on the fallibilities of the system and attempts to address the problem. Borchard's work famously identified the most typical errors by highlighting the cases of 82 people who had been wrongfully convicted. His findings are now canonical for innocence advocates and are referenced in most academic, journalistic, and legal writing on the issue. His list of causes included:

- Mistaken eyewitness identification.
- Reliance on circumstantial evidence (frequently accompanied by perjury).
- "Carelessness or overzealousness" by the prosecutors.
- "Zealousness" or gross negligence by the police.
- Prejudicial inferences are drawn from the prior record of the person accused of the crime.
- False confessions.
- Unreliable "expert" evidence.
- Inadequate defence because 'the accused were poor persons.'

Borchard's writings informed the approaches of innocence projects and advocates nearly 50 years later. His influence is still apparent, as innocence projects routinely publish factors from his exploratory list under their 'causes of wrongful conviction' on their website as a form of public advocacy and policy lobbying (see Innocence Project 2024c; Florida Innocence Project 2024). For example, the outstanding work of The National Registry of Exoneration (2024) routinely releases reports of exoneration that categorise cases under *five* or *six* contributing factors that help audiences understand the perversity of wrongful convictions within fallible systems. While useful in broader policy advocacy and political pressure, reducing the complexity and intersectionality of wrongful conviction has flattened out the experience of the innocent and simplified their experiences in pursuit of broader justice for all.

Along with informing advocacy, Borchard's work was highly influential on a new lineage of wrongful conviction research that has been drawn towards empirical studies linked to causation (Leo, 2017). It was the first to implement an often-replicated 'inductive method of drawing wrongful conviction causes' from the case narrative (Zalman, 2020, p. 137). Perhaps influenced by American criminological paradigms and legal research preferences toward empiricism, the Borchardian approach has created a list of evidentiary or causal factor errors that, in turn, generate policy reforms that may address the issue. Whether these points are framed as causes of wrongful conviction or contributing factors, research in this space has expanded scholarly recognition of the problem and created avenues to explore it in more depth (Leo, 2005; Norris & Bonventre, 2015; Leo, 2017). However, despite recognition of the need to expand, this approach reduces wrongful conviction to a small subset of legal and evidential issues that remove anything outside of courtroom evidence, such as socio-cultural biases and marginalisations, from the explanation of error.

One factor influencing this absence rests in the methodology commonly employed in innocence research. Since wrongful conviction, particularly the "actual innocence" with which many researchers are enamoured, can only be analysed post-exoneration, our understanding of these issues is inherently biased. Relying on exonerations to understand how wrongful convictions occur limits our perspective to the most visible issues, allowing us only to understand the tip of the iceberg in relation to error. Because wrongful conviction is rarely corrected, given the best estimates at between 3% and 5% of serious offences, examining these successes may only offer a glimpse into errors implicating the innocent. In this sense, the overzealousness of academics to understand wrongful conviction via the retrospective analysis of successful exonerations or identified near misses offers a form of survival bias that cannot fully explore the entire story of wrongful conviction.

Survival biases occur when researchers focus on entities that have successfully passed a selection process while neglecting those that have not (Mangel & Samaniego, 1984). In this case, researchers tend to focus on those successfully exonerated or 'innocent' rather than on those who have been wrongfully convicted. This bias can lead to skewed conclusions and misunderstandings about the factors contributing to success or failure (Mangel & Samaniego, 1984). While the contribution of this work to the knowledge surrounding wrongful conviction cannot be understated, the combination of the early momentum of the DNA-led exonerations and retrospective academic analysis of error may have limited our understanding of the issue, particularly outside the borders of the United States.

Adjusting Wrongful Conviction Analysis

To grasp the full extent of wrongful conviction, it is essential to look beyond the visible successes of exoneration and consider the issues pertinent to the often-unseen failures to exonerate. As advocates for the wrongfully convicted, we need not look at only the successes nor the just so-called near misses where the innocent are acquitted or have charges dropped prior to trial (Gould et al., 2013; Norris et al., 2020). While this may give us additional insight into what has happened, it does not go far enough. Given the lower rates of exoneration in non-US jurisdictions, the knowledge about wrongful convictions is already less complete and requires alternative avenues to understand potential solutions. For this reason, the experience of working on unsuccessful or in-progress claims of wrongful conviction enables us to explore a more comprehensive recognition of the influences of error and the barriers faced by the innocent. These claims may be made in public via the media, news, journalistic inquiry, and even true crime. The understanding may come from innocence projects where hundreds of applications are received and cases reviewed, but only a small minority progress to any system recognition and even fewer through to successful exoneration. Often left out of wrongful conviction explorations are court acquittals, where innocence may not be conclusively found, but doubt about a conviction remains.

A more comprehensive approach allows for a more accurate and nuanced understanding of the risks that expose the innocent. This approach enables a continuation of the analysis of successful exonerations but also respects the experiences of those who have had failed attempts to assist them. The approach to wrongful conviction risks in this way complements and expands the tradition of examining wrongful conviction as a retrospective analysis defined by legal success. It deviates by disregarding academic conventions about 'innocence' to explore wrongful conviction through other lens including personal narratives and claims of error that legal systems may not recognise as innocence or, despite evidence to the contrary, consider guilty. Existing approaches often overlook the possibility that the wrongfully convicted are not always exonerated. Given the limited success in overturning errors in non-US jurisdictions, this may ultimately lead to more informed decisions and strategies in investigating, advocating, and appealing claims of innocence.

Our suggested approach is not without its challenges. Wrongful conviction and 'actual' innocence have been tightly defined within academic circles in attempts to make sense of the problem. The contestation and theoretical gymnastics around who is recognised as 'innocent' or 'exonerated' is a great assist in quantifying wrongful conviction. It was duly important in an era where scepticism surrounded the existence and prevalence of wrongful conviction. Again, the work of the US National Registry of Exonerations has been crucial for quantifying the extent of error in the United States. Despite these efforts, arguments have regularly been raised regarding the validity of the wrongfully convicted as 'innocents' or 'wrong man errors' (Leo, 2017). The contestation exists because some, like the National Registry of Exonerations (2024), define an exoneree as someone who 'was convicted of a crime and later officially declared innocent of that crime, or relieved of all legal consequences of the conviction because evidence of innocence that was not presented at trial required reconsideration of the case.' Additional definitional caveats include requiring that an 'exoneree' be declared factually innocent by a government authority, have received a pardon, or have had all charges dismissed or acquitted.

While the Registry's definition is broad, it has also conflated terms like exoneree, innocence, and wrongful conviction. For some, these caveats beyond being declared 'factually innocent' represent a problem for innocence, as we cannot be definitive about the individual's claim to a wrongful conviction. In some sense, this debate exposes the motive behind the use of the data. The concerns over its representativeness of the 'truly' innocent rest in an empiricist's eye for detail and objective truth (Leo, 2017). For advocates, the expansive dataset and analysis provide insight into areas requiring policy reform and change. However, both only offer retrospective analysis based on a definition of error identified via varying exoneration definitions.

Our suggested approach of identifying the risks, interconnectedness, and overlapping factors that contribute to wrongful conviction rather than solely examining their causes does not inherently distinguish between a genuinely innocent person and a guilty person claiming to be a victim of the system. For wrongful conviction purists, this approach is incompatible with attempts to quantify morally justifiable support for the innocent. It often clashes with the traditions of the innocence work we participate in, which has gained valuable academic and procedural insights into the specific faults experienced by those navigating the system. However, it opens new benefits for research by enabling an examination of the cases and experiences of all those claiming to be wrongfully convicted to expand our cumulative knowledge about the gaps, flaws, and problems in a system which is rarely accessed by advocates and researchers.

This approach extends alternative methods that have been an emerging focus of researchers over the past decade. It emphasises the need for a more expansive exploration of why wrongful convictions occur, rather than limiting the focus to analysing past errors. Self-report studies of people who are currently incarcerated have become one option used to examine the full extent of potential errors, often illustrating a significantly higher error rate than the long-held assumption of 3–5% (Gudjonsson et al., 2021; Loeffler et al., 2019). While obvious flaws are presented when using self-report studies, the innovative approach has recognised significant failures in less serious offences, which are rarely the focus of discussion. By including these offender categories in the analyses of potential wrongful convictions, these studies highlight the need for greater insight, innovation, and advocacy for those convicted of less serious offences in the academic examination of their experiences.

Similarly, the view that perspectives on wrongful convictions have been overly narrow is not uncommon. Reflecting on 30 years of wrongful conviction advocacy in the US, Robert Norris et al. (2020) recognised areas that were overlooked in the DNA exoneration era during the early 2000s, including those referred to as the 'Elephants in the Courtroom'. Among these concerns are the relationship between race and wrongful convictions, 'false' guilty pleas, and the unacknowledged 'misdemeanour' wrongful convictions (Norris et al., 2020). This work highlights the need to broaden wrongful conviction scholarship by expanding research in the 'circle of harms' associated with wrongful conviction to ensure we better understand their causes, lived experiences, and long-term consequences. Despite these insights, the continued reliance on definitional boundaries around wrongful conviction highlights how the needs of the innocent can be entangled and subjugated to the academic tendencies to define, categorise, and pigeonhole rather than understand the problem. Importantly, these are the same concerns we have in presenting the argument in this book. By no means do we want to be definitive in our examination of influences or create borders about how wrongful convictions occur.

We are cognisant of work in the US that has begun exploring the 'circles of harm' surrounding wrongful conviction (Norris et al., 2020). For example, Janani Umamaheswar (2023) has written about the 'racialised cumulative disadvantage' of wrongful conviction that understands the issue beyond the evidence presented at trial that could convict or exonerate. Umamaheswar (2023) recognised how wrongful convictions of Black and Hispanic men are produced because of intersecting and accumulating inequalities and socioeconomic, psychological, and emotional harms. Unbound by legal academic tendencies to define, quantify, and categorise wrongful conviction, Umamaheswar's work is part of a new wave of researchers and advocates attempting to address the issue by moving beyond hindsight reflection to understand the social, cultural, psychological, economic, and political influences that position some to be particularly vulnerable to miscarriages of justice. To understand and provide solutions to wrongful convictions, we need to move beyond the cases where innocence can be conclusively established to ensure we gather a complete picture of the cumulative practices that result in a miscarriage of justice.

The Limits of Innocence

It should be noted that we are writing this book from the unique perspective of academics working within the Bridge of Hope Innocence Initiative at RMIT University in Melbourne, Australia. Established in 2014, the Initiative follows the tradition of other innocence projects around the world. Much like every other innocence project in Australia, our dedicated team and students have not at the time of writing, progressed a case to the stage of 'exoneration' despite multiple legal appeals, applications, and petitions to governments. In the over 20 years since the first innocence project was established at Griffith University in Queensland and the formation of multiple university and non-university innocence projects, the absence of 'exonerations' in Australian innocence work has significant consequences. For all our efforts, innocent people remain in prison, while some are now living in the community with the continued hope of clearing their name. Our experiences have recognised a raft of issues in the Australian criminal justice system that creates risk for wrongful convictions, but a lack of collective success hinders our advocacy for the justice reforms needed to help innocent people we know exist.

The absence of success in Australia is not without hope or evidence of significant flaws in the criminal justice system. Our work with the Innocence Initiative has identified issues linked to potential wrongful convictions from non-disclosure (Ruyters et al., 2021), police investigation tactics (Ruyters & Bartle, 2024), and systemic racism and bias (MacFarlane & Stratton, 2016; Stratton & Sigamoney, 2023). These insights have come from our experiences dealing with hundreds of applications. We have publicly advocated for some of these cases due to our frustrations with the mechanics of the Australian system and the need for public information to move our investigations forward. These experiences, combined with acknowledged wrongful conviction cases such as Folbigg, reassure us that the issue is as pertinent as anywhere else in the world.

These experiences are why we see limitations in the current approach to wrongful conviction outside the US. While there have been 30 years of rekindled knowledge and awareness resulting from the DNA exoneration revolution, this is not enough. The relevance of the existing work has created a two-fold issue for international innocence advocates. The first is that the work has tended to emphasise that wrongful convictions (at least in specific cases) can be reduced to a specific moment in the criminal justice system. Cases tend to be discussed in relation to the issue they presented—for example, police misconduct—rather than the breadth of errors and experiences that the innocent face.

The reduction of wrongful convictions towards singular issues has led to somewhat of a cottage industry of distanced academic research on these errors, rather than helping the wrongfully convicted. Formal and informal research consortiums have emerged around causal factors such as forensic science error, eyewitness error, and interviewing techniques, but with little practical involvement in assisting with claims of innocence. These consortiums have more in common with laboratory-style approaches to scientific research or even policing studies than advocacy for the wrongfully convicted. Despite this, they continue to lobby and position research funding with presumed advocacy for the wrongfully convicted.

While this research is crucial for providing a better understanding of the human element, the distance from actual wrongful convictions has become an issue for innocence advocacy. The detachment of these researchers from real cases and their focus on specific errors that align with their interests, rather than addressing the cumulative and diverse experiences of the wrongfully convicted, limits better recognition of the innocent and the development of strategies or institutions to rectify these gross errors.

Rather than representing the experiences of the innocent, the causal factors emphasised by distanced researchers often have little connection to people who claim to have experienced or been harmed by a wrongful conviction. Instead, these researchers, often unaware, are dependent on new errors in the system to further their work and promote solutions based on their findings and beliefs. Furthermore, the success of this work in the US has created a bounded reality that advocates for system reform to limit future errors rather than to identify current mistakes.

These approaches have led to the second issue, which is that this knowledge has created an ecosystem in which innocence has been narrowly defined by using successful cases and creating an orthodoxy of legal terminology and outcomes. This innocence ecosystem creates a bottleneck in which there is a disconnect between the issues experienced by the innocent and the reliance on 'successful cases' that navigated the complexities of the criminal justice system. As a result, legal scholars, socio-legal academics, scientists, and policy decision-makers often view wrongful convictions through a narrow lens of the limited, singular issues apparent in these successes, rather than the faults in the many more failed, incomplete, and in-progress claims of innocence.

The problem is not so much the focus of distanced research that has not engaged with a wrongful conviction claim but the intensity of advocacy around this myopic view of system error resulting from this research. For example, the intense focus on scientific error has positioned discussions around racism in police investigations as a secondary effect of wrongful conviction rather than its primary definer. Discussions about Farah Jama's wrongful conviction, which is discussed later in this book, are usually always about the forensic error that led to his conviction rather than the casual racism of the police and prosecution who chose to prosecute the case based on the single DNA sample. As a result, the intense focus of science reform advocacy on explaining and addressing wrongful convictions through purely scientific methods has often usurped the struggles of those who cannot be helped by scientific evidence. This has been parlayed into advocacy for system reform and institutional development in the post-conviction review space, such as conviction integrity units and criminal justice review commissions, which look solely and forensically at available evidence rather than understanding the systemic and social issues that may contribute to wrongful convictions. While any mechanism is better than none, we recognise the need for intersectional responses that cover evidential misgivings in cases and the more problematic elements experienced in society.

This distance has yet to encompass views from those with experience in managing claims of innocence. Advocates like innocence projects offer a more robust and broader ecology of wrongful conviction understanding. Zeroing in on single issues discounts complexities such as prior criminal history, family life, and psychological and mental health, which are left unrecognised by the existing approach. Part of the difficulty for policymakers, decision-makers, and legal scholars is that wrongful conviction is not only a legal nor a criminal justice fault. Wrongful conviction is often incorporated within social, political, and cultural structures that enact injustice outside the courtroom and formal structures. Racism, sexism, religious persecution, marginalisation, and vulnerability are acknowledged in wrongful conviction literature, but the reliance on addressing mechanisms within the system rather than understanding social and cultural pressures has meant that system reform has been unable to address these problems. It is no accident that jurisdictions often viewed as the most racially segregated are overrepresented both in the imprisonment rates of minorities and in the miscarriages of justice. Like the US experience, Australian states presenting similar issues of marginalisation also faced the most significant issues of injustice related to deaths in custody, police inquiries, and other markers of systemic violence and racism.

Research must examine system factors which are often unavailable to the unaware, distanced, wrongful conviction researcher. Where there is an acknowledgement of issues such as legal aid, inadequate defence, and courtroom inequities, the distanced research paradigm has been used to examine these issues in a more finite and granular fashion. Often, these issues are bundled as inadequate defence or prosecutorial misconduct without examining the perspective of the wrongfully convicted about why their story was not believed. Much of the field focuses on legal scholarship, which may explain why research has tended to explore wrongful convictions from a system professional standard and training perspective rather than a human story about bias, assumptions, and prejudice. This perspective attempts to explain courtroom errors via similar operational variable explanations, such as eyewitness recall and memory errors.

For this reason, we attempt in this book to persuade innocence advocacy to move beyond the wrongful conviction purist and distanced research paradigm. The book forwards an understanding of wrongful conviction that prioritises the experiences of those working with the wrongfully convicted every day. This approach acknowledges the impact of the research and advocacy that came before it but also recognises that the thousands of case files, letters, interviews, and conversations passing through innocence projects provide a very different understanding of wrongful conviction.

This discussion leads to our primary aim of developing the argument in the book. To improve screening mechanisms, investigations, and institutional responses to wrongful convictions, we need better research and a better understanding of the influences, causes, and factors that contribute to wrongful convictions. Part of our reason for exploring this has been the typical presentation of wrongful conviction as an amorphous error in Australia. Typically, no one is held accountable, and there is little systemic reaction or response, which frustrates the recognition of the problem.

How to Approach This Book

This book is not a proposal to theorise wrongful convictions as some have done under systems, ecological, or other theories to make sense of the problem (Crump, 2024). Nor does it stand in any way as a critique of these attempts. Instead, this book aims to reveal the striking number of risks posed by the criminal justice system for the innocent. It does this to assist current and future recognition of these risks to support the claims of the innocent, while encouraging reform in areas that enable these risks, particularly outside of the US.

For this reason, upon approaching this book, it will become obvious that we have avoided some common elements that have come to define wrongful conviction scholarship. One notable absence is the lack of a definitional element of wrongful conviction. A plethora of academic contestations already exist about who the term "wrongfully convicted" represents. Similarly, innocence and exoneration rest in contestable spaces in academic realms and for innocence movements. We are not exploring who the wrongfully convicted are or how wrongful convictions are defined in this book. Rather, we look at the risks that may lead to wrongful convictions. In this way, while we frame these risks as pertinent to wrongful convictions, these risks apply to the 'actual factual' innocent and procedural issues that lead to questionable outcomes within a trial. For these reasons, this book is not about wrongful conviction cases in Australia, although we do refer to known cases that illustrate the issues we have identified from time to time.

Linked to the lack of adherence to any definitional dogma is an absence or reframing of causal factors or categories. As we mentioned earlier, the inability of causal factor research to connect these issues outside of the US experience is a sign of the need for a step back towards a more holistic and specific representation of what contributes to wrongful conviction in Australia and potentially around the world. The aim is to move forward discourse that helps those claiming to be innocent and limits future error and helps our ability to respond and recognise wrongful conviction. This book is not intended as a checklist for distanced academics seeking new sites of research or as a tool for practitioners to absolve themselves by assuming it will eliminate the possibility of error in a case. Instead, it represents an opportunity to raise awareness of the potential faults, flaws, and issues about which practitioners and advocates must be aware to ensure that wrongful convictions do not occur. This book is about recognising the existence of these risks to improve the pre- and post-conviction landscape for the innocent.

While we are not seeking to add to definitional boundary discussions, we need to explain how we use the terms "wrongful convictions" and "miscarriages of justice" in this book. We use the term 'miscarriages of justice' in its legal context. In Australia, a miscarriage of justice is one of the grounds on which convictions can be overturned on appeal (see e.g., *Criminal Appeal Act 1912* (NSW) s 6(1)). Where convictions are overturned on that basis, they are described as wrongful. We use "wrongful conviction" to refer to established or suspected wrongful convictions and the risks of wrongful conviction created by the systemic, social, and structural issues we discuss in the following chapters.

Using this approach, we have structured the book into chapters that attempt to make better sense of wrongful conviction. Chapter 2 expands on existing wrongful conviction scholarship to build on attempts to categorise how wrongful conviction occurs. Rather than continue with a list of factors that individualise error, this chapter proposes that wrongful conviction requires recognition of the multiple risks and elements that contribute to error. In proposing this, the chapter frames the remainder of the book to encourage researchers and practitioners to focus their work on the many structural, systemic and cultural errors, negligence, and lack of oversight that come to form wrongful convictions. Through eight short chapters, we demonstrate how a confluence of risks expose the potential for wrongful convictions across many more cases than we are currently able to identify in Australia.

Chapter 3 introduces the influence of subjective cultures and the risk of different types of bias in decision-making by criminal justice professionals that can result in error. Following this chapter, we discuss what we view as the risks of wrongful conviction. The risks we identify demonstrate the fragilities of the justice system, whether they are human or policy-induced but are not to be considered silos in any way. Chapter 4 explores the critical role of the conduct of criminal justice professionals has shaping the problematic outcomes of criminal trials. We look at how misconduct and systemic failures by police, prosecutors, defence counsel, and forensic experts contribute to wrongful convictions. Chapter 5 explores vulnerabilities in how evidence is managed from the investigation stage through to its presentation in court, exposing a significant risk of wrongful conviction. Chapter 6 considers the risks associated with the use of what is often unreliable forensic science and identification evidence. Chapter 7 extends the critique of evidence by examining the risks created through failures in understanding through language and cognitive disadvantage, a lack of English capacity, and misinterpretation of demeanour or silence. Similarly, Chap. 8 recognises the risks in our system's reliance on confessional evidence and guilty pleas that are influenced by structural incentives rather than the pursuit of truth. Chapter 9 follows the recognition of structural incentives and aims as influences on wrongful conviction by demonstrating the impact of insufficient funding, which limits defence lawyers' ability to dedicate adequate time to case preparation and investigation in a system that is increasingly burden by an increase in the volume of evidence presented in a modern case. Chapter 10 bookends the analysis of risk by emphasising how the criminal justice system's emphasis on managerialism to expedite procedures has created a heightened potential for error among the most vulnerable people in our communities.

Finally, Chap. 11 offers a short conclusion to the identification of risk and wrongful conviction. Emphasising the need to stimulate research and practice to gather a greater understanding of the many influences and risks that contribute to wrongful convictions in Australia. We conclude by suggesting the need for greater emphasis on four critical intersecting risks for wrongful conviction in Australia, which we hope will stimulate debate and research.

Cases

Folbigg v The King [2023] NSWCCA 325

Legislation

Criminal Appeal Act 1912 (NSW)

References

Bathurst, T. (2022). *2022 Inquiry into the convictions of Kathleen Megan Folbigg. N. Government.* https://2022folbigginquiry.dcj.nsw.gov.au/content/dam/dcj/2022-folbigg-inquiry/documents/Report_of_the_2022_Inquiry_into_the_convictions_of_Kathleen_Megan_Folbigg.pdf

Borchard, E. M. (1932). *Convicting the innocent: Errors of criminal justice.* Yale University Press.

Blewer, R., Weathered, L., Dioso-Villa, R., & Murakami, J. (2023). Miscarriages of justice in Australia. In *Murder, wrongful conviction and the law* (pp. 185–200). Routledge.

Brohus, M., Arsov, T., Wallace, D. A., Jensen, H. H., Nyegaard, M., Crotti, L., Adamski, M., Zhang, Y., Field, M. A., Athanasopoulos, V., Baró, I., Ribeiro de Oliveira-Mendes, B. B., Redon, R., Charpentier, F., Raju, H., DiSilvestre, D., Wei, J., Wang, R., Rafehi, H., Kaspi, A., Schwartz, P. J., et al. (2021). Infanticide vs. inherited cardiac arrhythmias. *Europace: European Pacing, Arrhythmias, and Cardiac Electrophysiology: Journal of the Working Groups on Cardiac Pacing, Arrhythmias, and Cardiac Cellular Electrophysiology of the European Society of Cardiology, 23*(3), 441–450. https://doi.org/10.1093/europace/euaa272

Cunliffe, E. (2011). *Murder, medicine and motherhood.* Bloomsbury Publishing.

Cordner, S., & Breen, K. (2023). *Wrongful convictions in Australia: Addressing issues in the criminal justice system.* Australian Scholarly Publishing.

Crump, T. G. (2024). An ecological understanding of wrongful convictions in the U.S. criminal justice system. *Cogent Social Sciences, 10*(1). https://doi.org/10.1080/23311886.2024.2421342

de Vinuesa, Carola Garcia. (2021). https://theconversation.com/kathleen-folbiggs-children-likely-died-of-natural-causes-not-murder-heres-the-evidence-my-team-found-156487

Dwyer, J., Neufeld, P. J., & Scheck, B. (2001). *Actual innocence: When justice goes wrong and how to make it right.* New American Library.

Florida Innocence Project. (2024). https://www.floridainnocence.org/contributing-factors

Garrett, B. L. (2020). Wrongful convictions. *Annual Review of Criminology, 3*(1), 245–259.

Godsey, M. (2017). *Blind injustice: A former prosecutor exposes the psychology and politics of wrongful convictions*. University of California Press.
Gould, J. B., Carrano, J., Leo, R. A., & Hail-Jares, K. (2013). Predicting erroneous convictions. *Iowa Law Review, 99*, 471.
Gould, J. B., & Leo, R. A. (2010). One hundred years later: Wrongful convictions after a century of research. *The Journal of Criminal Law and Criminology*, 825–868.
Gudjonsson, G. H., Gonzalez, R. A., & Young, S. (2021). The risk of making false confessions: The role of developmental disorders, conduct disorder, psychiatric symptoms, and compliance. *Journal of Attention Disorders, 25*(5), 715–723. https://doi.org/10.1177/1087054719833169
Hamer, D., & Dwyer, A. (2023). *Australia needs a dedicated body for wrongful convictions*. https://www.sydney.edu.au/news-opinion/news/2023/06/06/australia-needs-a-dedicated-body-for-wrongful-convictions.html.
Innocence Project. (2023). *DNA exonerations in the United States (1989–2020)*. https://innocenceproject.org/dna-exonerations-in-the-united-states/.
Innocence Project. (2024a). *About*. https://innocenceproject.org/about/
Innocence Project. (2024b). *Exonerations data*. https://innocenceproject.org/exonerations-data/
Innocence Project. (2024c). *The issues*. https://innocenceproject.org/the-issues/
Le, L. C., Hoang, Y. H., Bui, H. T., Nguyen, D. Q., Mai, S. T., & Luong, H. T. (2023). Wrongful convictions in Asian countries: A systematic literature review. *International Journal of Comparative and Applied Criminal Justice*, 1–17.
Leo, R. A. (2005). Rethinking the study of miscarriages of justice: Developing a criminology of wrongful conviction. *Journal of Contemporary Criminal Justice, 21*(3), 201–223.
Leo, R. A. (2017). The criminology of wrongful conviction: A decade later. *Journal of Contemporary Criminal Justice, 33*(1), 82–106. https://doi.org/10.1177/1043986216673013
Loeffler, C. E., Hyatt, J., & Ridgeway, G. (2019). Measuring self-reported wrongful convictions among prisoners. *Journal of Quantitative Criminology, 35*, 259–286.
Mangel, M., & Samaniego, F. J. (1984). Abraham Wald's work on aircraft survivability. *Journal of the American Statistical Association, 79*(386), 259–267. https://doi.org/10.2307/2288258
MacFarlane, J., & Stratton, G. (2016). Marginalisation, managerialism and wrongful conviction in Australia. *Current Issues in Criminal Justice, 27*(3), 303–321. https://doi.org/10.1080/10345329.2016.12036048
Medwed, D. S. (2017). Talking about a revolution: A quarter century of DNA exonerations. In D. S. Medwed (Ed.), *Wrongful convictions and the DNA revolution: Twenty-five years of freeing the innocent* (pp. 2–13). Cambridge University Press.

National Registry of Exonerations. (2024). https://www.law.umich.edu/special/exoneration/Pages/about.aspx

Norris, R., & Bonventre, C. L. (2015). Advancing wrongful conviction scholarship: Toward new conceptual frameworks. *Justice Quarterly, 32*(6), 929–949.

Norris, R. (2017). *Exonerated: A history of the innocence movement*. NYU Press.

Norris, R. J., Acker, J. R., Bonventre, C. L., & Redlich, A. D. (2020). Thirty years of innocence: Wrongful convictions and exonerations in the United States, 1989-2018. *Wrongful Conviction Law Review, 1*, 2.

Norris, R. J., Bonventre, C. L., & Acker, J. R. (2021). *When justice fails: Causes and consequences of wrongful convictions*. Carolina Academic Press.

Robins, J. (Ed.). (2023). *Murder, Wrongful Conviction and the Law. An international comparative analysis*. Taylor & Francis.

Ruyters, M., Stratton, G., & Bartle, J. (2021). The culture of non-disclosure and miscarriages of justice. *Alternative Law Journal, 46*, 299–306.

Ruyters, M., & Bartle, J. (2024). Who's watching Mr. Big? Scenario operations and induced confessions. *Current Issues in Criminal Justice, 36*(3), 318–333. https://doi.org/10.1080/10345329.2024.2305986

Stratton, G., & Sigamoney, A. (2023). Why we don't see race: How Australia has overlooked race as an influence on miscarriages of justice. *Race and Justice, 13*(2), 256–271. https://doi.org/10.1177/2153368720922294

Umamaheswar, J. (2023). Wrongful conviction as racialized cumulative disadvantage. *The British Journal of Criminology, 63*(3), 537–552.

Zalman, M. (2020). Edwin Borchard's innocence project: The origin and legacy of his wrongful conviction scholarship. *Wrongful Conviction Law Review, 1*, 124.

CHAPTER 2

Risk Rather than Causes: Expanding Understandings of Wrongful Conviction

Abstract In this chapter, we argue for a necessary shift in how we understand wrongful conviction. Rather than individualising 'causes', we emphasise the interconnected risks embedded within the criminal justice system that coalesce to produce miscarriages of justice. We contend that traditional approaches emerging from the United States tend to individualise error, often focusing on factors like false confession, and fail to adequately address the deeper structural, systemic, and social faults at play. Outside of the US, experiences like those of Gene Gibson typify a more complicated understanding of error. A vulnerable young Aboriginal man with significant cognitive and linguistic challenges, Gibson's case starkly illustrates how multiple failures across individuals, systems, and institutions can subvert justice. Our approach moves beyond a search for a single 'cause' to present a broad constellation of risks, which are categorised under the overarching themes of culture and practice, capacity and capability, and transparency and accountability. By examining wrongful conviction through this risk-based lens, the book aims to provide a more nuanced framework for identifying and mitigating the conditions that render cases vulnerable to error.

Keywords Wrongful conviction • Risk factors • Systemic faults • Structural faults • Culture • Practice • Capacity • Capability • Transparency • Accountability

M. Ruyters et al., *Innocence Unveiled*,
https://doi.org/10.1007/978-3-031-91343-3_2

In 2010, the death of 21-year-old Josh Warneke in remote northwest Western Australia led to an investigation titled 'Operation Aviemore'. In 2012, Gene Gibson, an 18-year-old Aboriginal man from the Western Desert community of Kiwirrkurra, was implicated in Warneke's death after he confessed to striking Warneke with a vehicle during an unrecorded police interview (*State of Western Australia v Gibson* 'Gibson' [2014] WASC 240) The unrecorded interview and a subsequent recorded interview were excluded before trial on the basis that they were not voluntary, had been obtained in breach of legislative requirements, and it would be unfair to admit them (*Gibson,* 2014, [183]). Despite this, Gibson pleaded guilty to manslaughter and was sentenced to seven years and six months' imprisonment. In 2017, however, Gibson successfully appealed his conviction in the Western Australia Court of Appeal on grounds that he had not sufficiently understood the nature and implications of the guilty plea due to his cognitive impairments, his very basic level of oral English, and his inability to read written English (*Gibson v The State of Western Australia* 'Gibson' [2017] WASCA 141, [137], [157]).

Gibson's case, which is discussed in more detail in the next chapter, exposed numerous causal factors, as well as additional experiences that represent significant risks of wrongful conviction. The combination of cognitive impairment and limited English proficiency had left Gibson unable to understand procedural elements in his navigation through the criminal justice system (*Gibson*, 2017 [157],[174] [163]. There were also significant issues relating to the lack of an independent interpreter in his interviews with police (*Gibson* 2014, [180]) and the adequacy of interpreting services provided up to his sentencing hearing, which included concerns that an interpreter embellished communications from Gibson's lawyer to Gibson (*Gibson*, 2017, [46],[168]–[169], [188]). The police officers who initially interviewed Gibson had not followed the "Anunga Rules" (*R v Anunga and Others* (1976) 11 ALR 412), which offer Indigenous people a range of protections such as the requirement for an interpreter when English proficiency is limited, acknowledgement of cultural requirements, and the presence of a "prisoner's friend" in an attempt to curtail false or coerced confessions (*Gibson,* 2014, [180]). The officers concerned had little experience in conducting interviews with Aboriginal people in remote Western Australia (Corruption & Crime Commission, 2015).

The case is a striking example of how structural, systemic, and cultural issues can coalesce against the wrongfully convicted to subvert their claims of innocence and any potential successful trial outcome. Gibson's case does not fit neatly into the causal or risk factor framework that has dominated wrongful conviction discourse for 30 years. The Western Australian Supreme Court of Appeal's overturning of Gene Gibson's conviction highlights the confluence of risk and vulnerabilities that contribute to miscarriages of justice in Australia, particularly those experienced by Indigenous people. Rather than identifying a single causal factor that led to Gibson's wrongfully conviction, his successful appeal and two Crime and Corruption Commission reports demonstrated how multiple people, systems, and institutions failed a vulnerable, young Indigenous man (Crime & Corruption Commission, 2015, 2018).

Gibson's experience is typical of many cases in Australia, where wrongful convictions represent a confluence of issues resulting in error and harm, which are retrospectively acknowledged. In cases like Gibson's, the typical approach to wrongful conviction has been to rely on factors such as false confession and unreliable witnesses to explain the imprisonment of the innocent (Garrett, 2020). For example, world-famous wrongful conviction cases such as the 'Central Park Five' are often reduced to issues in evidence such as false confessions rather than systemic racism and media pressure (Stratton, 2015). The continual deference to a small list of factors individualises or compartmentalises error rather than reflect multiple risks and elements that inflict harm on innocent people. Where individual causal factors have often been the focus of legal and criminological research, the evidence suggests that many structural, systemic and cultural errors, negligence, and lack of oversight culminate in wrongful convictions.

Structural, Systemic, and Social Faults and Wrongful Conviction

Identifying wrongful convictions exposes faults and risks in criminal justice systems, which are often interconnected. The widespread failure of the system to deliver justice often stems from a complex network of relationships between systemic mechanisms, actors, and individual agency that makes identifying an individual fault often difficult. Miscarriages of justice occur because the various arms of the criminal justice system are inadequate to identify and trigger awareness of potential errors early enough to stop them from occurring. However, one benefit of systemic faults leading to wrongful conviction is that because they exist within the system's machinery, each is potentially fixable. When systems do not work, institutional reforms can often identify and fix the issue.

Systemic faults often arise from complex interdependencies, making them difficult to predict and manage. For example, issues of false confession and the unreliability of eyewitness evidence have been identified as fundamental causes of wrongful conviction around the world (Garrett, 2020; Gudjonsson, 2012). Social and cultural elements influence their collection, but the errors associated with these forms of evidence emerge as a systemic problem because of the system's reliance on evidence. Systemic risks are risks that can trigger widespread failures across interconnected elements within the justice system. For example, the absence of an interpreter to ensure a suspect's linguistic presence can have ripple effects as a case progresses through the system, leading to the development of a problematic case.

The system's mechanisms for verifying accuracy may also be insufficient, suggesting sizeable flaws in the effective functioning of a 'just' criminal justice system. A further issue is the lack of accountability for decision-making by criminal justice professionals, such as the police, which can lead to significant errors. These issues are often framed in canonical literature as misconduct leading to wrongful convictions. Scrutiny of these actions, however, is often limited by gaps in accountability and oversight processes, a lack of transparency, poor decision-making, rare gross misconduct, and systems that protect these actors from liability in case of error (Equal Justice Project, 2024).

Structural faults represent potential problems that stem from inherent weaknesses in the economic, political, and institutional structures governing society. For example, deficiencies in critical infrastructure, such as underfunded legal aid, prosecution budgetary constraints, and poorly designed forensic lab protocols, can undermine the system's capacity to function correctly or fairly. Weak or poorly enforced regulations can lead to an increased risk of error due to structures not providing adequate support for the innocent. Structural faults can also arise within organisations from internal pressures, such as time constraints or cultural norms. For instance, different rules and policies regarding evidence preservation and access to evidence for testing can create structural faults, which impede proving a person's innocence. Even when evidence of innocence is obtained or obtainable, police and prosecutors may resist re-examining the evidence or reopening the case due to structural factors within the justice system.

Structural faults also emerge through pressures within organisations, such as time pressures to complete investigations, organisational cultures that promote efficiency over thoroughness, and a system belief in finality rather than truth. These kinds of pressures can result in resistance to re-examining cases, even when compelling proof of wrongful conviction is presented. Legislative and judicial resistance to review can also compound the systemic problem of wrongful convictions by preventing the correction of past mistakes. In essence, structural factors, influenced by internal organisational pressures, can initiate and exacerbate systemic issues within the justice system, leading to a cascade of negative consequences for the innocent.

Wrongful conviction disproportionately impacts those in society who are the most marginalised, vulnerable, and disadvantaged, often perpetuating further injustice in their lives. The social dynamics and interactions that significantly impact communities are exposed when innocent people are convicted of crimes they did not commit. Social issues such as racism, sexism, inequality, discrimination, poverty, and mental health inequity contribute to what can be referred to as 'social determinants of justice' (McCausland & Baldry, 2023). While these social determinants have been used to highlight the increasing risk of justice system contact, a broad range of social factors disproportionately increases the risk of wrongful convictions. The evidence of these influences on wrongful conviction is plentiful, whether that is reflected in data from The National Registry of Exonerations that Black people were seven times more likely to be wrongly convicted of murder than innocent white people (Gross et al., 2022) or that women are often wrongfully convicted for a crime that never occurred (Jackson & Gross, 2014).

Again, these social issues are not faults in themselves and certainly not categories of causation. With this said, social risk faults play a significant role in wrongful convictions and demonstrate an intersection with systemic and structural faults. People from marginalised and vulnerable backgrounds face a higher risk of wrongful conviction due to various social faults that arise through structural responses, including biased prosecution and limited access to quality legal representation. Systemic elements intersect with social elements in the over-surveillance of specific communities, and lack of access to well-resourced legal representation, limited access to diversionary options and bail, and inadequate specialist services, further exacerbating the risk of wrongful convictions. For example, the Montana Innocence Project (2024) recognises that people living in poverty are disproportionately represented in the criminal justice system and are more likely to be wrongfully convicted due to the shortcomings of the public defender system. Their experience highlights the intersectionality of these risks in explaining how poverty, heavy caseloads, and inadequate government funding contribute to miscarriages of justice (Montana Innocence Project, 2024). In a similar relationship between social and systemic elements, pretrial elements such as denial of bail and plea bargains disproportionately impact the most marginalised in the community. Gross et al. (2022) demonstrate that Black and Latinx accused are more likely to be detained pretrial, increasing vulnerability associated with employment, housing, and family stability. A systemic element that often remains unacknowledged is that the promise of a plea bargain allowing immediate release creates a strong incentive for an innocent person to plead guilty (Petersen, 2020; Cheng, 2013). This structural incentive has had a significant impact on wrongful convictions in the US, with nearly 25% of those exonerated since 1989 pleading guilty and nearly 75% of these from racially marginalised groups (Gross et al., 2022).

Categorising Wrongful Conviction Risk

The current understanding of the source of wrongful convictions has relied on retrospective analysis of comparatively few cases where the innocent have been exonerated via post-conviction review. However, outside the United States, the innocent often struggle to overturn their wrongful conviction, and the path to exoneration is less clear, requiring a reframing of analysis that can assist in identifying and correcting miscarriages of justice. Importantly, this is not a process of retrospectivity to find the cause of error to collate for further regression analysis. Instead, it reflects the experience of innocence projects in Australia and elsewhere to demonstrate that the causal factors often associated with errors are not the only barriers to justice. Instead, we frame the issue of wrongful conviction under the risks that leave any case vulnerable to a miscarriage of justice.

This approach aligns with Rossmo and Pollock's 'sentinel events perspective' of wrongful conviction. In this approach, a sentinel event is a significant negative outcome that signals underlying weaknesses in a justice system or process and results from compounding errors (National Institute of Justice, 2017). Notably, in the context of the arrangement we present in this book, a sentinel event analysis can provide essential frameworks for strengthening the system and preventing future adverse events or outcomes (National Institute of Justice, 2017). Using a sentinel event framework, Rossmo and Pollock (2019) explained that wrongful convictions highlight significant failures across multiple interrelated causes that are individual failures but also indicative of deeper structural issues. In advocating for the sentinel event approach, they separated an approach from other forms of the justice system failure that focus on enabling procedural and policy improvements but do little to limit wrongful convictions. Rossmo and Pollock (2019, p. 794) note the limitation of the standard approach to factors of wrongful conviction as a tactic that:

> can uncover errors, it does little to prevent them. The effort to assign responsibility and blame to a particular person can also produce obfuscation and denial by those who attempt to deflect blame or defend themselves from sanctions.

Our approach is not framed by sentinel event analysis, nor does it rely on confirmation bias, for example, as a single fulcrum of error. It aligns, however, with the benefit of determining the situations that create error rather than a 'linear' approach to determining the causes. The risks identified in this work can act as a potential warning to advocates about detecting, avoiding, or mitigating the risk of wrongful convictions. Both approaches are sceptical that wrongful convictions have a single 'causal bottom line' and that attempts to categorise cases in that way do little to recognise the risk of error or prevent future problems.

For this reason, we present a broad array of risks for wrongful conviction, not as categories of causation but as a constellation or coalescence of vulnerability to error. Broadly, we use the concepts of culture and practice; capacity and capability; and transparency and accountability. Each of these overlaps with systemic, structural, and social elements within the criminal justice system to organise our overall insight of the wide spectrum of risks in this space. For example, in some instances, police misconduct may be considered a singular 'causal' issue. However, misconduct is a layered, multi-faceted issue intersecting systemic pressures on police, their socialisation through training, institutional issues of racism and sexism, and structural mechanisms that mask bad behaviour behind laws and processes. In the following sections, we explain how we understand these concepts for the purposes of this book.

Culture and Practice

Occupational culture, a sociological concept, refers to the shared beliefs, values, and practices that shape the behaviour and interactions of individuals within a workplace (Sackmann, 1991). It aims to explain the intersection of culture, knowledge, and the operation of workplaces. Within the workplace, a 'cultural knowledge map' creates an internal cultural setting that includes a range of accepted practices, understandings, languages, and expectations (Sackmann, 1991). Importantly, a single occupational culture often does not exist in workplaces, with 'subcultures' emerging underneath a broader overlay of an occupational culture (Sackmann, 1992). This splintering can result in competing practices and objectives within the same organisation. For example, legal cultures exist as stable patterns of legally oriented behaviour and attitudes but exist in different contexts across the legal system (Nelken, 2017). It can encompass various elements, including 'facts' about institutions, such as the role of lawyers and the appointment of judges, to more nebulous ideas, values, aspirations, and mentalities towards law, justice, and the processes they entail (Nelken, 2017). These cultures exist on micro and macro levels and overlap with similar formulations of occupational cultures, including prosecutors (Dunlea, 2022), defence (Welsh & Newman, 2024), law firms (Chambliss, 2010), judicial (Maroney, 2011), and police (Chan, 1997; Loftus, 2009; Reiner, 2010).

The intersection of these cultures can create 'complex ensembles of values, attitudes, symbols, rules, recipes, and practices' (Reiner, 2010, p. 116). These behaviours are not embedded within institutions; rather, they emerge through the work and practices of the people within them. As a result, practices such as prosecutorial compassion (Vaynman & Fondacaro, 2022), prosecutorial colourblindness (Dunlea, 2022), and judicial dispassion (Maroney, 2011) emerge not as simple requirements of the job or even predispositions of the people in those roles. Instead, they emerge through the practices of individuals and groups that become enmeshed in the culture of the organisation.

Organisational culture and practice in criminal justice systems are not necessarily problematic but expose significant risks. As with any culture, risks emerge when culture and practice go unquestioned and become assumed elements of the job and organisation. Again, these can be inert, even helpful in some instances, but also expose a risk towards bias and error in justice and wrongful conviction. Take, for example, the emergence of defence and law firm cultures that have been demonstrated to exhibit a range of elements, including camaraderie and standardisation among their staff (Welsh & Newman, 2024). Each of these elements comes to define these legal cultures but also highlights risks that may conflict with the role of providing an adequate defence or prosecution during a trial. Criminal defence work is inherently cooperative, involving teamwork or informal networks among defence lawyers, prosecutors, judges, and police across various jurisdictions (Welsh & Newman, 2024). Despite their differing roles, prosecutors and defenders often form informal networks that facilitate collaboration within the criminal justice system that, while beneficial, also create an environment lacking oversight. Similarly, in the current underfunding of legal aid that plagues more jurisdictions, legal cultures have seen a standardisation of service that considers the routinisation of practice in criminal defence. This mechanisation, driven by funding pressures and the need to handle large caseloads, negatively impacts lawyer-client relationships, resulting in perceptions of the justice system as merely a 'production line' for convictions that open the potential for error and injustice (Welsh & Newman, 2024).

System Capacity and Individual Capability

Criminal justice systems are flawed in their nature, with constant competition between efficiency and procedure influencing everyday outcomes (Kubrin & Tublitz, 2022). The drive for efficiency is evident in phenomena such as 'backward pressure', which refers to a reduced capacity to process cases through the system to reduce the flow of cases to subsequent stages (Bernard et al., 2005). There is an ongoing rate of attrition between overworked police, the cases they have resources to investigate, the cases that prosecutors are resourced to prosecute, and the capacity of the courts to hear them. This results in an emphasis on discretional decision-making at each stage, reducing the system's ability to act to its full capacity.

Often, we discuss capacity in terms of state institutions being unable or unwilling to prosecute, particularly in relation to failures to respond adequately to gendered and family violence (Hamilton et al., 2023; Myhill & Johnson, 2016). Questions over the system's function emerge in the inability to address core functions of ensuring justice and accountability, just as they do when the innocent are convicted of crimes they did not commit. The failure to address these justice concerns is exposed in systems worldwide that are working over capacity at a significant cost to victims and the community (Mears, 2017). The concept of system capacity becomes helpful in understanding that the criminal justice system has a responsibility to achieve justice and meet that objective. Capacity, in this sense, could refer to the ability of police to follow procedural protections or courts to provide timely outcomes while achieving fair and just outcomes for the community. While capacity may seem imbued within institutions like police and courts, it can only exist when practiced and performed. Capacity, in this sense, 'thrives and survives on practice, repetition, exploration, conjecture, and refutation' (Appadurai, 2004, p. 69). When practices are subsumed by cultural influences and biases that clash with their objectives, the capacity to deliver justice is reduced even further.

From the perspective of wrongful conviction, the capacity of a system and its actors working at capacity builds pressure. Criminal justice agencies face the dual risk of being perceived as incompetent if too many cases reopen—either due to reoffending or public dissatisfaction—or if they fail to close enough cases overall (Bernard et al., 2005). This dynamic can lead to hasty or inadequate case resolutions, increasing the likelihood of wrongful convictions. Ultimately, criminal justice professionals who cannot effectively manage their caseloads and ensure that cases remain closed may be identified as incompetent, perpetuating a cycle that undermines the justice system's integrity.

The system's capacity to deliver justice often faces strains that tragically intersect with the capabilities of the innocent to navigate and engage with it. Inherent in the concepts of access to justice and the right to a fair trial is the ability of defendants to communicate effectively, understand the different stages of the proceedings against them, and understand the implications of decisions they are asked to make. Too often, cognitive and language impairments coalesce with social risks and a system working beyond capacity. In the example we referred to earlier, Gene Gibson's lawyer had difficulties arranging an interpreter for their meetings. Gibson's first language was Pintupi, but only two Pintupi interpreters were available due to under-resourcing, while the Aboriginal Legal Service (WA) was also 'significantly stretched' (*Gibson,* 2017, [132]). Consequently, several conversations between Gibson and his lawyer took place in English without the assistance of an interpreter. Capability is often overlooked in rule of law frameworks which assume accessible and fair processes when the reality is that people experiencing disabilities, such as cognitive or hearing impairments, are effectively excluded from participating in their own case (Lundberg & Simonsen, 2015, p. 8).

Transparency and Accountability

Criminal justice systems possess the democratically delegated authority to use force on the presumption that force will ensure safety and justice. Given that criminal justice personnel have the authority to use force, impose penalties, and restrict liberty, their actions must be transparent and subject to scrutiny to ensure they act within ethical and legal boundaries (Prenzler, 2021). Concepts of transparency and accountability help maintain public trust and legitimacy, ensuring that the powers granted to these individuals are exercised responsibly and justly.

Transparency rests as an operative concept that has come to define contemporary institutions. We currently live in an 'age of transparency' (Owetschkin et al., 2021) defined by the social and political requirements for institutional and social transparency, the disclosure of and unimpeded access to information, the revelation of secret dealings, and public oversight over political life and the economy. These elements are said to translate to the criminal justice system, where transparency and disclosure in police investigations and trials are core tenets (Ruyters et al., 2021). Miscarriages of justice become a more significant risk when mechanisms such as police or prosecutions abdicate their responsibilities to ensure these protections are upheld (Ruyters et al., 2021).

Some protections for the defendant exist as fundamental ideals of the due process. However, even in an age of transparency, many criminal justice agencies resist the idea that the public should play a role in their oversight (Geraghty & Velez, 2011). Where many government organisations are increasing their transparency, criminal justice agencies continue to deny and resist access to police records, decision-making outcomes in parole hearings, and even sentencing outcomes in lower courts (Geraghty & Velez, 2011). The lack of transparency works against the contemporary conceptualisation of public scrutiny of institutions, particularly when discussing unchecked power and financial burden on the community (Owetschkin et al., 2021).

Where the criminal justice system holds individuals accountable for crimes through criminal prosecution, trial, and penalties via law, it ideally holds itself accountable via multiple mechanisms and oversight. Accountability in criminal justice encompasses two key aspects: performance, which relates to the effectiveness of the agency in achieving its goals, and conduct, which focuses on the ethical behaviour and integrity of its members (Prenzler, 2021). For instance, police accountability involves not only crime reduction and law enforcement but also the maintenance of ethical conduct (Prenzler, 2021). The system is further responsible for the rights of victims, potential victims, and the state itself. In the increasing absence of transparency, but often to enhance it, the criminal justice system defers to accountability structures to ensure institutions and individuals have checks and balances to curtail their power and influence. For this reason, the system often relies on accountability mechanisms to hold the police and courts answerable and to give the public an account of failure or error.

Cases

R v Anunga and Others (1976) 11 ALR 412
Gibson v The State of Western Australia [2017] WASCA 141
State of Western Australia v Gibson [2014] WASC 240

References

Appadurai, A. (2004). The capacity to aspire: Culture and the terms of recognition. In V. Rao & M. Walton (Eds.), *Culture and public action* (pp. 59–84). Stanford University Press.

Bernard, T. J., Paoline, E. A., III, & Pare, P. P. (2005). General systems theory and criminal justice. *Journal of Criminal Justice, 33*(3), 203–211.

Chambliss, E. (2010). Measuring law firm culture. In A. Sarat (Ed.), *Special issue law firms, legal culture, and legal practice (studies in law, politics, and society)* (Vol. 52, pp. 1–31). Emerald Group Publishing Limited. https://doi.org/10.1108/S1059-4337(2010)0000052004

Chan, J. B. L. (1997). *Changing police culture: Policing in a multicultural society.* Cambridge University Press.

Cheng, K. K. Y. (2013). Pressures to plead guilty: Factors affecting plea decisions in Hong Kong's magistrates' courts. *British Journal of Criminology, 53*(2), 257–275.

Corruption and Crime Commission, Report on Operation Aviemore: Major Crime Squad Investigation into the Unlawful Killing of Mr Joshua Warneke (Report, Corruption and Crime Commission, 5 November 2015).

Corruption and Crime Commission, The implementation of recommendations arising from the commission's investigation into operation Aviemore (Report, Corruption and Crime Commission, 4 April 2018).

Dunlea, R. R. (2022). "No idea whether he's Black, White, or purple": Colorblindness and cultural scripting in prosecution. *Criminology, 60*(2), 237–262.

Equal Justice Project. (2024). Retrieved from https://eji.org/issues/wrongful-convictions/

Garrett, B. L. (2020). Wrongful convictions. *Annual Review of Criminology, 3*(1), 245–259.

Geraghty, S., & Velez, M. (2011). Bringing transparency and accountability to criminal justice institutions in the South. *Stanford Law & Policy Review, 22*, 455.

Gibson -v- The State of Western Australia (2017) WASCA 141.

Gross, S. R., Possley, M., Otterbourg, K., Stephens, K., Weinstock Paredes, J., & O'Brien, B. (2022). *Race and wrongful convictions in the United States 2022.*

Gudjonsson, G. H. (2012). False confessions and correcting injustices. *New England Law Review, 46*, 689.

Hamilton, G., Ridgway, A., Powell, A., & Heydon, G. (2023). *Family violence and sexual harm: Research report.*

Jackson, M., & Gross, S. R. (2014). *Female exonerees: Trends and patterns.* Retrieved from https://www.law.umich.edu/special/exoneration/Pages/Features.Female.Exonerees.aspx

Kubrin, C. E., & Tublitz, R. (2022). How to think about criminal justice reform: Conceptual and practical considerations. *American Journal of Criminal Justice, 47*, 1050–1070. https://doi.org/10.1007/s12103-022-09712-6

Loftus, B. (2009). Police occupational culture: Classic themes, altered times. *Policing and Society, 20*(1), 1–20. https://doi.org/10.1080/10439460903281547

Lundberg, C., & Simonsen, E. (2015). Disability in court: Intersectionality and rule of law. *Scandinavian Journal of Disability Research, 17*(Sup 1), 7–22.

Maroney, T. A. (2011). The persistent cultural script of judicial dispassion. *California Law Review, 99*, 629.

McCausland, R., & Baldry, E. (2023). Who does Australia lock up? The social determinants of justice. *International Journal for Crime, Justice and Social Democracy, 12*(3), 37–53. https://doi.org/10.5204/ijcjsd.2504

Mears, D. P. (2017). *Out-of-control criminal justice: The systems improvement solution for more safety, justice, accountability, and efficiency.* Cambridge University Press.

Montana Innocence Project. (2024). Retrieved from https://mtinnocenceproject.org/race-and-poverty/

Myhill, A., & Johnson, K. (2016). Police use of discretion in response to domestic violence. *Criminology & Criminal Justice, 16*(1), 3–20.

National Institute of Justice. (2017). *Sentinel events initiative.* Retrieved from https://nij.ojp.gov/topics/articles/sentinel-events-initiative#whatis

Nelken, D. (2017). Using the concept of legal culture. In *Legal theory and the social sciences* (pp. 279–303). Routledge.

Owetschkin, D., Sittmann, J., & Berger, S. (2021). Cultures of transparency in a changing world – An introduction. In S. Berger, S. Fengler, D. Owetschkin, & J. Sittmann (Eds.), *Cultures of transparency* (pp. 1–14). Routledge.

Petersen, N. (2020). Do detainees plead guilty faster? A survival analysis of pretrial detention and the timing of guilty pleas. *Criminal Justice Policy Review, 31*(7), 1015–1035.

Prenzler, T. (2021). *Ethics and accountability in criminal justice: Towards a universal standard.* Australian Academic Press.

Reiner, R. (2010). *The politics of the police* (4th ed.). Oxford University Press.

Rossmo, K., & Pollock, J. (2019). Confirmation bias and other systemic causes of wrongful convictions: A sentinel events perspective. *Northeastern University Law Review, 11*(2).

Ruyters, M., Stratton, G., & Bartle, J. (2021). The culture of non-disclosure and miscarriages of justice. *Alternative Law Journal, 46*(4), 299–306. https://doi.org/10.1177/1037969X20987009

Sackmann, S. (1991). *Cultural knowledge in organizations.* Sage.

Sackmann, S. A. (1992). Culture and subcultures: An analysis of organizational knowledge. *Administrative Science Quarterly, 37*(1), 140-10.2307/2393536

Stratton, G. (2015). Transforming the Central Park jogger into the Central Park Five: Shifting narratives of innocence and changing media discourse in the attack on the Central Park jogger, 1989–2014. *Crime, Media, Culture, 11*(3), 281–297.

Vaynman, A. D., & Fondacaro, M. R. (2022). Prosecutorial discretion, justice, and compassion: Reestablishing balance in our legal system. *Stetson Law Review, 52*, 31.

Welsh, L., & Newman, D. (2024). Camaraderie and conflict: Developing an occupational culture typology of publicly funded criminal defence lawyers in England and Wales. *International Journal of the Legal Profession, 31*(1), 21–52.

CHAPTER 3

Subjective Cultures: Attitudes, Beliefs, and Values in the Justice System

Abstract This is the first of four chapters that consider intersecting cultures and practices within the justice system. This chapter explores the pervasive influence of subjective cultures, defined by normative beliefs and shared behavioural expectations, within the justice system. We examine how cognitive and social biases, as products of a dynamic interplay between societal and organisational levels, present a risk at every stage of the criminal justice process. Our analysis explores specific manifestations of bias in policing, prosecutorial impartiality challenges, and the susceptibility of judges and forensic experts to both cognitive and implicit social biases. The chapter highlights the association of tunnel vision with wrongful convictions and its impact on defence, policing, and prosecutorial practices. Finally, we identify the critical role of racism and racial bias as significant contributors to over-representation within the Australian criminal justice system and wrongful convictions.

Keywords Bias • Subjective culture • Tunnel vision • Racism and racial bias • Judicial exceptionalism • Prosecutorial impartiality

Culture is defined as the 'normative beliefs (i.e. system values) and shared behavioural expectations (i.e. system norms) in an organization' (James et al., 2008, p. 21). The subjective elements of culture are those social and

M. Ruyters et al., *Innocence Unveiled*,
https://doi.org/10.1007/978-3-031-91343-3_3

cognitive aspects of life, such as beliefs, attitudes, norms, and values (Triandis, 2002, p. 3). Triandis described subjective culture as society's 'characteristic way of perceiving its social environment' (Triandis, 2002, p. 3). These cultural behaviours are reproduced through socialisation as people learn how they should interact within their groups (McCarthy, 1998, p. 169). Subjective cultures are shaped by intergroup contact with people who share similar perspectives (Triandis, 1972), which can lead to the normalisation of prejudice and discrimination through these interactions (Andrade et al., 2023, p. 2). Racial profiling practices by police, for instance, may come to be seen as a routine part of their work (Chan, 2011, p. 76; Satzewich & Shaffir, 2009, p. 201) and be difficult to shift as a result.

We see culture as dynamic and dichotomous, operating at social and organisational levels which continually influence and shape one another. Cultural dynamics within organisations, such as the police, for instance, are shaped by the societal cultures in which individual police officers live, as well as organisational expectations, norms, and objectives. We are particularly interested in bias as a cultural product of this dynamic interplay.

The chapter begins by examining the omnipresence of bias, a pervasive aspect of human cognition and social interaction (Commission, 2021a). The risk of biased decision-making is present at every stage of the criminal justice process; cognitive and social biases are documented phenomena in police investigations, prosecutorial and juridical decision-making as well as in the observations of witnesses. Cognitive biases, described as a person's 'intuitive preferences', are systematic patterns of thinking, which can lead to errors in judgment (ALRC, 2021a, p. 7). These include confirmation bias, the 'tendency to interpret information in a way that confirms and reinforces pre-existing beliefs and opinions', and egocentric bias, which is the tendency to make self-serving judgements (Commission, 2021a, p. 7–8). Cognitive biases such as confirmation bias and tunnel vision are often grounded in occupational norms that can lead to errors in judgement and decision-making, and both are well-recognised contributors to wrongful convictions in studies outside Australia (Findley & Scott, 2006; Rossmo & Pollock, 2019). Rossmo and Pollock's study of potential criminal investigative failures found confirmation bias present in 80% of 43 wrongful conviction cases (2019, p. 802). Explicit and implicit social biases and cultural beliefs, especially those relating to gender, ethnicity, and race, are also known contributors (Katzman & Kovera, 2023; Lewis & Sommervold, 2014; Rizer III, 2002).

In the following sections, we look at the risk of different types of bias in decision-making by criminal justice professionals.

Policing Bias: Guardians of Justice

Research in Europe and the United States supports the vulnerability of police to confirmation bias (Meterko & Cooper, 2021; Kerstholt & Eikelboom, 2007; Wallace, 2015). Studies of police interview practices have consistently shown that police officers often presume that suspects are guilty prior to interviewing them, aiming primarily to obtain confessions rather than considering alternative perspectives (Hill et al., 2008). This presumption potentially biases the methods used to evaluate the credibility of suspects' statements, such as scientific content analysis ("SCAN") (Bogaard et al., 2014), which is addressed further in Chap. 11. While there is little research on the susceptibility of Australian police to confirmation bias, there is clear recent evidence that police decision-making in Australia is influenced by racial and LGBTIQ biases, which can lead to flawed investigations and potential wrongful convictions. The recent Special Commission of Inquiry into LGBTIQ hate crimes in NSW was tasked with investigating hate crimes actuated by LGBTIQ bias and considered the role of conscious and unconscious bias in the process of police investigations. During the Inquiry, the NSW Police Force (NSWPF) conceded that it was likely that conscious or unconscious bias influenced some of the cases considered by the Inquiry (Sackar, 2023, p. 1418). Hopkins and Popovic's analysis of police stops in Victoria also revealed a strong link between race and police decision-making and that racial appearance was a trigger for police intervention (Hopkins & Popovic, 2024). Weatherburn and Thomas similarly found that young Indigenous defendants are more likely than non-Indigenous young defendants to be prosecuted rather than cautioned for caution-eligible offences (Weatherburn & Thomas, 2023). We consider the impact of bias and racial over-representation in the criminal justice system further in this chapter.

Prosecution Bias: Ministers of Justice

The rule against bias requires impartiality in decision-making by judges and other public officials (Groves, 2021, p. 566; *Webb & Hay v The Queen* (1994) 181 CLR 41). Prosecutors are the gatekeepers of the criminal justice process, deciding which cases move forward to trial. They carry dual responsibilities as advocates for the State and as ministers of justice who must act fairly and impartially (Plater & Line, 2012, p. 58). The duty to act fairly is integral to their role and fundamental to the principles of a fair trial (Plater & Line, 2012, p. 61). All Australian jurisdictions have prosecution guidelines, emphasising prosecution obligations to act impartially and fairly (e.g., Office of the Director of Public Prosecutions, New South Wales, 2021). Established allegations of prosecution bias are rare, but bias can appear incidentally through processes such as jury selection. In *R v Smith,* a case of an Indigenous defendant, the trial judge discharged a jury because of the possible perception of bias after the prosecutor challenged the only three Indigenous jurors based on their Aboriginality (Anthony & Longman, 2017, p. 30; Rees, 1982).

When prosecutors fail to act objectively, decisions about whether to pursue charges may be influenced by extraneous factors, leading to weak circumstantial cases that are reliant on prosecution case theories proceeding to trial. Prosecution decision-making has recently come under scrutiny in Australia following judicial criticism. In one example, the NSW Director of Public Prosecutions ordered a review of sexual assault cases in March 2024 after criticism from several judges that the public prosecution office was prosecuting cases without merit (Dole, 2024). In the previous year, the Victorian Director of Public Prosecutions faced heavy criticism for deciding not to pursue charges against Victorian Police officers and others involved in using a lawyer as a police informant—a practice implicated in numerous potential miscarriages of justice (Estcourt & Vedelago, 2023).

Judicial Bias: Arbiters of Justice

Judicial impartiality is central to public confidence in the administration of justice and is a significant consideration for appeal courts and other oversight bodies (ALRC, 2021b, p. 3). The test for apprehended bias is whether a 'fair-minded observer' might reasonably apprehend that a judge may not bring 'an impartial and unprejudiced mind to the resolution of the question' (*Webb v The Queen* (1994) 181 CLR 41, p. 67, Deane J). Prompted by a decision in *Charisteas v Charisteas* (2020) 389 ALR 296 in relation to private communications between the judge and one of the parties, the Australian Law Reform Commission released a report in 2022 on judicial impartiality. The report considered, amongst other matters, the extent to which judges can 'resist bias' (Commission, 2021b, p. 6). There was some reason for concern given that some studies have found a potential for judges to overestimate their abilities to avoid bias in their decision-making, including in their assessment of the credibility of witnesses (Guthrie et al., 2009; Rachlinski et al., 2007; Rachlinski et al., 2008; Sagiv, 2015).

While many people demonstrate some egocentric bias (Ross & Sicoly, 1979), egocentric bias in judges can constrain their self-awareness of their own limitations, potentially leading to significant errors in decision-making. The importance placed on judicial impartiality may also make judges susceptible to perceptions of exceptionalism, namely, the belief that they have a greater capacity for objectivity than the public because of their extensive training and experience (Edmond & Martire, 2019, p. 633; Prescott, 2020, p. 116; Steiner-Dillon, 2019, p. 208). Exceptionalism assumes an imperviousness to bias (Edmond & Martire, p. 633), which suggests that judges are probably not in the best position to evaluate their own impartiality (Commission, 2021b).

Judges can also be influenced by implicit social and cultural biases, which can compromise impartial decision-making (Guthrie et al., 2002; Landsman & Rakos, 1994; Rachlinski et al., 2008). In an appeal against a sentence for soliciting in *Were v Police* [2003] SASC 116, Perry J noted inappropriate comments made by the sentencing magistrate, which included the words:

> You can go to work. Seven million of us do it whilst 14 million like you sit at home watching *Days of our Lives* smoking your crack pipe and using needles and I'm sick of you sucking us dry.
>
> Little Johnnie taxes us with all sorts, and now with salt tax and maybe war tax. We dicks pay for your life. It's your choice to be a junkie and die in the gutter. No one gives a shit, but you're going to kill that woman who is your mother, damn you to death. ([10])

While not addressing the clear bias apparent in the magistrate's comments, Perry J commented on the magistrate's 'diatribe' expressed in abusive terms on social and other issues not germane to the case before him' ([13]). Unabashed comments like this in a public court raise questions about the extent of implicit and less overt bias.

Expert Bias

Forensic experts are also susceptible to cognitive biases as part of their analysis, particularly confirmation bias (Cooper & Meterko, 2019), which occurs when experts consciously or unconsciously seek information that supports their pre-existing expectations or hypotheses. This can lead to errors, which undermine the reliability of their conclusions. Forms of analysis that rely on subjective interpretation and pattern recognition, such as blood stain pattern analysis as well as fingerprint comparison, are particularly susceptible to cognitive biases. These biases can influence how evidence is perceived and interpreted, potentially resulting in flawed analyses and false conclusions (Dror & Cole, 2010). For instance, the case of Gordon Wood, which is discussed in Chap. 6, illustrates how bias may have played a role in the expert's evidence. There is increasing awareness of the potential impact of cognitive bias on decision-making in the forensic sciences and the need for mitigating measures to reduce its influence (Dror, 2017; Edmond et al., 2017; Camilleri et al., 2019).

Tunnel Vision

Cognitive distortions, such as confirmation bias, hindsight bias, and outcome bias, play a significant role in the formation of tunnel vision, which can distort our perceptions and the conclusions drawn from them (Findley, 2010a, p. 6). In the criminal justice system, tunnel vision refers to a concentrated focus on a particular conclusion about a person, incident, or theory to the extent that other explanations or possibilities are disregarded. This process causes police, prosecutors, judges, and defence lawyers to interpret information about the case in ways that support their original conclusion (Findley & Scott, 2006; Martin, 2001) or persevere with beliefs despite contradictory evidence (Brants, 2013). Tunnel vision is sometimes equated with confirmation bias (see e.g. Hamer, 2015; Rassin, 2018), while other writers distinguish or attribute a causal link between both biases (e.g. Dror et al., 2011; Elaad, 2022; Findley, 2010b; Snook & Cullen, 2008). According to Elaad: '[t]unnel vision is over-reliance on internal sources while ignoring accurate external information. Confirmation bias is over-reliance on external sources that are not necessarily accurate…[b]oth operate simultaneously and might affect each other' (Elaad, 2022, p. 2).

While its prevalence in wrongful convictions is hard to quantify, tunnel vision is associated with many causal and risk factors leading to wrongful convictions (Findley & Scott, 2006; Gould et al., 2013). Of itself, tunnel vision is not generally a viable ground for overturning a conviction but is implicated in identified causes of wrongful conviction, such as witness identification error, false confessions, prison informer evidence, and police and prosecutorial misconduct (Findley, 2010a, 2010b; Martin, 2001). The concept of tunnel vision helps to explain the error snowball effect, namely that an initial error can trigger subsequent mistakes which culminate in a wrongful conviction (Findley & Scott, 2006; Gould et al., 2013; Leo & Drizin, 2010). The impact of tunnel vision is most pronounced in the police investigation stage, as their decision-making and information-gathering pervades the subsequent stages of the criminal justice process (Findley & Scott, 2006).

Tunnel Vision in Policing

In policing contexts, tunnel vision narrows police investigations to a single suspect. Police become so focused on a particular person or outcome that they are blind to other explanations and only select evidence and interview witnesses that tend to confirm that person as the suspect. Tunnel vision can also result from media or political pressure to find a viable suspect (Rossmo & Pollock, 2019). Tunnel vision affects what is seen as evidence, the scope of the investigation, the kinds of questions they might ask witnesses, and who is identified as a 'victim' a 'suspect', 'a witness' or a person of no interest. In *R v Ernst* [2020] QCA 150, for example, the appellant was convicted of sexual offences. The complainant's friend informed police that the complainant was having an affair with the appellant and had a propensity to lie, matters which were relevant to the complainant's credit, and the question of consent. This information was not noted or communicated to the prosecution and consequently was not disclosed to the defence. The appeal was granted, the court noting that [36]:

> ...[a]ccording to his evidence led on this appeal, the police officer's attention was only upon facts that might assist the prosecution case. He was only interested to find out if Ms V might be able to give evidence to strengthen the credit of the complainant. He was uninterested in learning that there may be issues about the reliability of the complainant and so he ignored (or did not hear) what Ms V had to say.

Tunnel vision can result in misconduct when police manufacture or curate evidence to meet their case theory, such as the improper nondisclosure practices by police in the case of Jason Roberts (IBAC, 2020) and the manipulation and withholding of evidence in the case of Andrew Mallard (Corruption and Crime Commission, 2008). In Jason Roberts' case, police investigating the murder of two police officers' fabricated evidence of two shooters being at the scene to match their case theory (*Roberts v The Queen* [2020] VSCA 58, [8]–[11]; *Roberts v The Queen* [2020] VSCA 277, [269]). In Mallard's case, which we discuss in more detail in Chap. 4, police failed to disclose that they tampered with forensic reports and changed key witness statements to strengthen their case against Mallard (*Mallard v The Queen* (2005) 224 CLR 125).

Prosecution Tunnel Vision

Tunnel vision can result in prosecutors emphasising evidence that fits their case theory while disregarding other relevant factors such as those that occurred in the case of Gordon Wood. For example, Gordon Wood was acquitted by the New South Wales Court of Criminal Appeal in 2012 of murdering his partner, Caroline Byrne, the court finding there was insufficient evidence to prove beyond reasonable doubt that Wood killed Byrne (*Wood v The Queen* [2012] NSWCCA 21. During Wood's subsequent unsuccessful suit for malicious prosecution, Fullerton J stated:

> The risk that a fixed view about the capacity of the available evidence, and the inferences it may support to establish the guilt of a person, might blind a prosecutor to his or her own failings of judgment as to how far to urge a jury to find guilt proved is obvious. It is equally obvious that a fixed attitude of that order might obscure deficiencies in the capacity of the evidence to prove guilt to the criminal standard. In discharging the high standards of fairness, objectivity and detachment by which a prosecutor is bound, a conscientious and self-reflective prosecutor is expected to modify any inclination to hold dogmatic views about the guilt of an accused and about the perceived strength of the Crown case in proof of guilt, in order to avert those risks. Those same expectations might, however, be displaced where a prosecutor has shown themselves to be arrogant or, as Mr Tedeschi's attitude in this case reveals, egoistic and defiant in the face of any challenge to the way he prosecuted the plaintiff, including adverse findings by the Court of Criminal Appeal [1336]

> I am left in no doubt that it was Mr Tedeschi's unerring belief in the rectitude of his own intellectual processes and prowess which dominated his decision to initiate and maintain the criminal prosecution of the plaintiff [1338]

On appeal, counsel for the state of New South Wales conceded that the prosecutor, Mark Tedeschi, had tunnel vision during the prosecution, focusing on flawed evidence 'to the exclusion of many other factors' (Whitbourn, 2019). The Court of Appeal, however, agreed with Fullarton J's conclusion that malice had not been proven (*Wood v State of New South Wales* [2018] NSWCA 313).

Tunnel Vision by Defence Lawyers

The concentration of defence lawyers and prosecutors on a particular case strategy is also recognised as a form of tunnel vision (Findley & Scott, 2006; Thomas III, 2007). For example, rather than calling any evidence, a defence trial strategy might be limited to challenging the prosecution case. Defence lawyers are not immune to cognitive biases, which can influence early decisions about the necessity of an interpreter for their client or whether certain witnesses will be called or questioned. Seeing cases as 'unwinnable' must inevitably influence some trial strategies (Sperling, 2010). Tunnel vision may also explain why defence lawyers fail to investigate their client's cases, assuming that the prosecution case is unassailable.

Racism and Racial Bias

Racial discrimination is a significant contributor to the over-representation of certain populations within criminal justice systems and can lead to race-based wrongful convictions (Free, 2017; Free & Ruesink, 2012; Gross et al., 2017; Smith & Hattery, 2011; Stratton & Sigamoney, 2023). In Australia, the over-representation of Indigenous people can be explained by racial inequalities and systemic racism across society and the justice system (Snowball & Weatherburn, 2008; Anthony & Blagg, 2012; Cuneen & Porter, 2017). The landmark Australian Royal Commission into Aboriginal Deaths in Custody ("Royal Commission") (1991) recognised longstanding racial discrimination as a significant factor, highlighting racialised approaches to policing and the susceptibility of policing to intensify towards Aboriginal people due to local law and order campaigns (Royal Commission, 1991). The findings illustrated how particular laws, processes, and institutional cultures disproportionately disadvantage Indigenous people in Australia, reflecting similar vulnerabilities experienced by racial minorities around the world (Free, 2017; Free & Ruesink, 2012; Gross et al., 2017; Smith & Hattery, 2011).

Racial over-representation often perpetuates perceptions of criminality or risk, resulting in practices informed by biased decision-making rather than evidence (Fitzgibbon, 2007; Hazlehurst & Dunn, 1988). For example, racial biases are reflected in law enforcement practices informed on the "prediction" of dangerous or "high-risk" groups, which often become accepted by individuals as generalisations about race and ethnicity (Chan & Chunn, 2014; Silver & Miller, 2002). These biases in Australia's history of racialised wrongful conviction have manifested in a prosecution based on a single piece of DNA evidence despite exculpatory evidence, as occurred in the case of Farah Jama (Vincent, 2010), and the use of incorrect interview tactics against racialised suspects. Further in the book, we consider the experiences of Farah Jama, Gene Gibson, Frank Button, and Kelvin Condren which resonate as examples where race is a prevalent issue in Australian wrongful convictions (Harrison & Trounson, 2021). These cases have illustrated how wrongful conviction is not only defined by errors, but also how decisions made by key figures in the criminal justice system have framed race as a central aspect of criminality (Taslitz, 2009; Majavu, 2018; Porter, 2018).

The racial biases these men faced, whether conscious or unconscious, systemic or individual, can lead to a disregard of a suspect's right to the presumption of innocence and conclusions of guilt based on their race, rather than a thorough examination of all available evidence (Stratton & Sigamoney, 2023). This over-representation can feed into perceptions that certain racial groups are inherently criminal, creating a climate of bias that influences miscarriages of justice like wrongful convictions. Unfortunately, racial bias and racism have rarely been acknowledged as an official influence on wrongful conviction and are equally difficult to retrospectively identify as systemic responses to these cases often blame broader issues like police training or confirmation bias, rather than individual or systemic racism (Stratton & Sigamoney, 2023).

Cases

Charisteas v Charisteas (2020) 389 ALR 296
Mallard v The Queen (2005) 224 CLR 125
R v Ernst [2020] QCA 150
Roberts v The Queen [2020a] VSCA 58
Roberts v The Queen [2020b] VSCA 277
Webb & Hay v The Queen (1994) 181 CLR 41
Were v Police [2003] SASC 116
Wood v The Queen [2012] NSWCCA 21
Wood v State of New South Wales [2018] NSWCA 313

References

Andrade, L. N., Torres, C. V., & Safdar, S. (2023). *"They can fight their own fights": Prejudice, permissiveness, and discrimination against minorities* (p. 39). Teoria e Pesquisa.

Anthony, T., & Blagg, H. (2012). *Addressing the crime problem of the northern territory intervention: Alternate paths to regulating minor driving offences in remote indigenous communities.* Report to the Criminology Research Council Grant: CRC 38/09-10. http://www.criminologyresearchcouncil.gov.au/reports/CRG_38-0910_FinalReport.pdf

Anthony, T., & Longman, C. (2017). Blinded by the White: A comparative analysis of jury challenges on racial grounds. *International Journal for Crime, Justice and Social Democracy, 6*(3), 25.

Australian Royal Commission into Aboriginal Deaths in Custody. (1991). *Royal commission into aboriginal deaths in custody: National reports* [vol. 1–5], and regional reports. Australian Government Publishing Service.

Bogaard, G., Meijer, E. H., Vrij, A., Broers, N. J., & Merckelbach, H. (2014). Contextual bias in verbal credibility assessment: Criteria-based content analysis, reality monitoring and scientific content analysis. *Applied Cognitive Psychology, 28*(1), 79–90.

Brants, C. (2013). 9 Tunnel vision, belief perseverance and bias confirmation: Only human? In *Wrongful convictions and miscarriages of justice* (pp. 161–192). Routledge.

Camilleri, A., Abarno, D., Bird, C., Coxon, A., Mitchell, N., Redman, K., Lindsay, H., et al. (2019). A risk-based approach to cognitive bias in forensic science. *Science & Justice, 59*(5), 533–543.

Chan, J. (2011). Racial profiling and police subculture. *Canadian journal of criminology and criminal justice = Revue canadienne de criminologie et justice pénale, 53*(1), 75–78. https://doi.org/10.3138/cjccj.53.1.75

Chan, W., & Chunn, D. (2014). *Racialization, crime, and criminal justice in Canada*. University of Toronto Press.

Commission, A. L. R. (2021a). *Judicial impartiality: Background paper J16 cognitive and social biases in judicial decision-making*. A. Government.

Commission, A. L. R. (2021b). *Review of judicial impartiality, Consultation paper and background papers. A. Government*. A. Government.

Cooper, G. S., & Meterko, V. (2019). Cognitive bias research in forensic science: A systematic review. *Forensic Science International, 297*, 35–46.

Cunneen, C., & Porter, A. (2017). Indigenous peoples and criminal justice in Australia. In A. Deckert & R. Sarre (Eds.), *The Palgrave handbook of Australian and New Zealand criminology, crime and justice*. Palgrave Macmillan. https://doi.org/10.1007/978-3-319-55747-2_44

Dole, N. (2024, 07/03/2024). NSW director of public prosecutions orders review of every sexual assault case committed for trial following criticism from judges. *ABC News*. https://www.abc.net.au/news/2024-03-07/nsw-sexual-assault-cases-trial-review/103556852

Dror, I. E., & Cole, S. A. (2010). The vision in "blind" justice: Expert perception, judgment, and visual cognition in forensic pattern recognition. *Psychonomic Bulletin & Review, 17*(2), 161–167.

Dror, I. E., Pascual-Leone, A., & Ramachandran, V. (2011). The paradox of human expertise: Why experts get it wrong. *The Paradoxical Brain, 177*.

Dror, I. E. (2017). Human expert performance in forensic decision making: Seven different sources of bias. *Australian Journal of Forensic Sciences, 49*(5), 541–547.

Elaad, E. (2022). Tunnel vision and confirmation bias among police investigators and laypeople in hypothetical criminal contexts. *SAGE Open, 12*(2), 21582440221095022.

Edmond, G., & Martire, K. (2019). Just cognition: Scientific research on bias and some implications for legal procedure and decision-making. *The Modern Law Review, 82*(4), 633.

Edmond, G., Towler, A., Growns, B., Ribeiro, G., Found, B., White, D., Martire, K., et al. (2017). Thinking forensics: Cognitive science for forensic practitioners. *Science & Justice, 57*(2), 144–154.

Estcourt, D., & Vedelago, C. (2023, 22/06/23). Top legal minds urge DPP to let jury decide Gobbo and police guilt. *The Age*. https://www.theage.com.au/politics/victoria/careful-and-realistic-public-prosecutor-defends-lack-of-lawyer-x-charges-20230622-p5diji.html

Findley, K. A. (2010a). Tunnel vision. In *Conviction of the Innocent: Lessons from Psychological Research*. APA Press.

Findley, K. A. (2010b). Tunnel vision. In B. Cutler (Ed.), *Convictions of the innocent: Lessons from psychological research*. APA Press, 2010, University of Wisconsin Legal Studies Research Paper No. 1116.

Findley, K. A., & Scott, M. S. (2006). Multiple dimensions of tunnel vision in criminal cases. *The Wisconsin Law Review, 291.*

Fitzgibbon, D. W. (2007). Institutional racism, pre-emptive criminalisation and risk analysis. *The Howard Journal of Criminal Justice, 46*(2), 128–144.

Free, M. D., Jr., & Ruesink, M. (2012). *Race and justice: Wrongful convictions of African American men*. Boulder.

Free, M. D., Jr. (2017). Wrongful convictions: The African American experience. *Race, Ethnicity and Law, 22*, 7–25.

Gould, J. B., Carrano, J., Leo, R. A., & Young, J. K. (2013). *Predicting erroneous convictions: A social science approach to miscarriages of justice*. University of San Francisco Law Research Paper (2013–20).

Gross, S. R., Possley, M., & Stephens, K. (2017). *Race and wrongful convictions in the United States.* National Registry of Exonerations. University of California Irvine.

Groves, M. (2021). Clarity and complexity in the bias rule. *Melbourne University Law Review, 44*(2), 565–601.

Guthrie, C., Rachlinski, J. J., & Wistrich, A. J. (2002). Judging by heuristic-cognitive illusions in judicial decision making. *Judicature, 86*, 44.

Guthrie, C., Rachlinski, J. J., & Wistrich, A. J. (2009). The "hidden judiciary": An empirical examination of executive branch justice. *Duke Law Journal*, 1477–1530.

Hamer, D. (2015). The Eastman case: Implications for an Australian criminal cases review commission. *Flinders LJ, 17*, 433.

Harrison, M., & Trounson, J. (2021). An investigation of the key factors leading to the wrongful conviction of Aboriginal and Torres Strait Islander peoples. *Journal of Australian Indigenous Issues, 24*(3–4), 20–36.

Hazlehurst, K., & Dunn, A. T. (1988). Aboriginal criminal justice. *Trends & Issues in Crime & Criminal Justice, 13.*

Hill, C., Memon, A., & McGeorge, P. (2008). The role of confirmation bias in suspect interviews: A systematic evaluation. *Legal and Criminological Psychology, 13*(2), 357–371.

Hopkins, T., & Popovic, G. (2024). Do Australian police engage in racial profiling? A method for identifying racial profiling in the absence of police data. *Current Issues in Criminal Justice*, 1–22.

Independent Broad-based Anti-corruption Commission. (2020). Operation Gloucester – An investigation into improper evidentiary and disclosure practices in relation to the Victoria Police investigation of the murders of Sergeant Gary Silk and Senior Constable Rodney Miller. V. G. Printer. ibac.vic.gov.au/publications-and-resources/article/operation-gloucester-special-report-july-2020

James, L. R., Choi, C. C., Ko, C. H. E., McNeil, P. K., Minton, M. K., Wright, M. A., & Kim, K. I. (2008). Organizational and psychological climate: A review of theory and research. *European Journal of Work and Organizational Psychology, 17*(1), 5–32.

Katzman, J., & Kovera, M. B. (2023). Potential causes of racial disparities in wrongful convictions based on mistaken identifications: Own-race bias and differences in evidence-based suspicion. *Law and Human Behavior, 47*(1), 23.

Kerstholt, J. H., & Eikelboom, A. R. (2007). Effects of prior interpretation on situation assessment in crime analysis. *Journal of Behavioral Decision Making, 20*(5), 455–465.

Landsman, S., & Rakos, R. F. (1994). A preliminary inquiry into the effect of potentially biasing information on judges and jurors in civil litigation. *Behavioral Sciences & the Law, 12*(2), 113–126.

Leo, R. A., & Drizin, S. A. (2010). The three errors: Pathways to false confession and wrongful conviction. *Police Interrogations and False Confessions: Current Research, Practice, and Policy Recommendations (American Psychological Association, 2010), Univ. of San Francisco Law Research Paper* (2012-04).

Lewis, A. L., & Sommervold, S. L. (2014). Death, but is it murder: The role of stereotypes and cultural perceptions in the wrongful convictions of women. *Albany Law Review, 78*, 1035.

McCarthy, E. (1998). The dynamics of culture, organisational culture and change. *AI & SOCIETY, 12*, 155–184.

Majavu, M. (2018). The 'African gangs' narrative: Associating blackness with criminality and other anti-black racist tropes in Australia. *African and Black Diaspora: An International Journal, 13*(1), 27–39.

Martin, D. L. (2001). Lessons about justice from the laboratory of wrongful convictions: Tunnel vision, the construction of guilt and informer evidence. *UMKC Law Review, 70*, 847.

Meterko, V., & Cooper, G. (2021). Cognitive biases in criminal case evaluation: A review of the research. *Journal of Police and Criminal Psychology*, 1–22.

Office of Director of Public Prosecutions New South Wales. (2021). *Prosecution guidelines*. In. New South Wales: Office of Director of Public Prosecutions New South Wales.

Plater, D., & Line, L. (2012). Has the 'silver thread' of the criminal law lost its lustre? The modern prosecutor as a minister of justice. *University of Tasmania Law Review, 31*(2), 55–95.

Porter, A. (2018). Non-state policing, legal pluralism and the mundane governance of "crime". *Sydney Law Review, 40*(4), 445–467.

Prescott, D. E. (2020). Bending the light of social science in family court: Epistemic injustice and epistemic exceptionalism matter. *The Journal of the American Academy of Matrimonial Lawyers, 33*, 99.

Rachlinski, J. J., Guthrie, C., & Wistrich, A. J. (2007). Heuristics and biases in bankruptcy judges. *Journal of Institutional and Theoretical Economics (JITE)/ Zeitschrift für die gesamte Staatswissenschaft*, 167–186.

Rachlinski, J. J., Johnson, S. L., Wistrich, A. J., & Guthrie, C. (2008). Does unconscious racial bias affect trial judges. *Notre Dame Law Review, 84*, 1195.

Rassin, E. (2018). Reducing tunnel vision with a pen-and-paper tool for the weighting of criminal evidence. *Journal of Investigative Psychology and Offender Profiling, 15*(2), 227–233.

Rees, N. (1982). R v Smith. *Aboriginal Law Bulletin.*

Rizer, A. L., III. (2002). The race effect on wrongful convictions. *William Mitchell Law Review, 29*, 845.

Ross, M., & Sicoly, F. (1979). Egocentric biases in availability and attribution. *Journal of Personality and Social Psychology, 37*(3), 322.

Rossmo, D. K., & Pollock, J. M. (2019). Confirmation bias and other systemic causes of wrongful convictions: A sentinel events perspective. *NEULR, 11*, 790.

Sackar, J. (2023). Special Commission of Inquiry into LGBTIQ hate crimes volume 3. S. C. o. I. i. L. h. crimes. https://www.nsw.gov.au/sites/default/files/2023-12/SCOI-LGBTIQ-Hate-Crimes-Volume-3-191223.pdf

Sagiv, M. (2015). Cultural bias in judicial decision making. *BCJL & Soc. Just., 35*, 229.

Satzewich, V., & Shaffir, W. (2009). Racism versus professionalism: Claims and counter-claims about racial profiling. *Canadian Journal of Criminology and Criminal Justice, 51*(2), 199–226.

Silver, E., & Miller, L. (2002). A cautionary note on the use of actuarial risk assessment tools for social control. *Crime and Delinquency, 48*(1), 138–161.

Smith, E., & Hattery, A. J. (2011). Race, wrongful conviction & exoneration. *Journal of African American Studies, 15*, 74–94.

Snook, B., & Cullen, R. M. (2008). Bounded rationality and criminal investigations: Has tunnel vision been wrongfully convicted? In *Criminal investigative failures* (pp. 95–122). Routledge.

Snowball, L., & Weatherburn, D. (2008). Theories of indigenous violence: A preliminary empirical assessment. *Australian and New Zealand Journal of Criminology, 41*, 216–235.

Sperling, C. (2010). Defense lawyer tunnel vision: The oft-ignored role defense counsel plays in wrongful convictions. *The Defender*(18–19).

Steiner-Dillon, J. R. (2019). Epistemic exceptionalism. *Indiana Law Review, 52*, 207.

Stratton, G., & Sigamoney, A. (2023). Why we don't see race: How Australia has overlooked race as an influence on miscarriages of justice. *Race and Justice, 13*(2), 256–271.

Taslitz, A. E. (2009). Wrongly accused redux: How race contributes to convicting the innocent: The informants example. *Southwestern University Law Review, 37*, 1091–1148.

Thomas III, G. C. (2007). *Solving the lawyer problem in criminal cases.*

Triandis, H. (1972). *The analysis of subjective culture.* Wiley.

Triandis, H. C. (2002). Subjective culture. *Online Readings in Psychology and Culture, 2*(2), 6.

Vincent, F. (2010). *Report: Inquiry into the circumstances that led to the conviction of Mr Farah Abdulkadir Jama* (Victorian Government Printer). http://www.justice.vic.gov.au/wps/wcm/connect/5a103e804263c8da810e832b0760a79a/VincentReportFinal6May2010.pdf?MOD¼AJPERES

Wallace, W. A. (2015). *The effect of confirmation bias in criminal investigative decision making.* Walden University.

Weatherburn, D., & Thomas, B. (2023). The influence of indigenous status on the issue of police cautions. *Journal of Criminology, 56*(2–3), 253–277.

Whitbourn, M. (2019, 19 November, 2019). *Prosecutor in Gordon Wood trial 'not ill-motivated', court told.* Sydney Morning Herald.

CHAPTER 4

Practice in the System: The Conduct of Criminal Justice Professionals

Abstract Following on from the previous chapter's discussion of the risks posed by subjective cultures, this chapter examines how intersecting cultures can create behaviours and practices among criminal justice professionals that shape miscarriages of justice. We begin by raising an expanded potential of police misconduct, including unethical practices, a results-driven culture, and specific examples like 'verballing', evidence tampering, and non-disclosure. The influence of police culture, often linked to corruption and a disregard for ethical conduct, is examined. The chapter also explores the role of prosecutors by clarifying the duties and ethical responsibilities of prosecutors and the distinction between misconduct and errors in judgement. The challenges and wide discretion afforded to defence counsel are also considered, along with the difficulty of overturning convictions based on tactical errors or perceived incompetence. Finally, the chapter addresses forensic misconduct and systemic issues within forensic institutions, highlighting instances of error, mismanagement, and potential bias.

Keywords Wrongful convictions • Police misconduct • Prosecutorial misconduct • Defence counsel • Forensic misconduct • Police culture • Non-disclosure

M. Ruyters et al., *Innocence Unveiled*,
https://doi.org/10.1007/978-3-031-91343-3_4

This chapter explores the critical role of criminal justice professionals in shaping the outcomes of criminal trials. We look at how misconduct, errors, and systemic failures by police, prosecutors, defence counsel, and forensic experts contribute to wrongful convictions. We open with a discussion of police conduct and well-worn themes of corruption, unethical practices, and a results-driven culture within police forces. While wrongful convictions resulting from prosecutorial misconduct are less common in Australia, we consider the duties of prosecutors, their ethical responsibilities, and the challenges arising in weak circumstantial cases. We also explore the role of defence counsel, focusing on the challenges of forensic decision-making, the consequences of inadequate representation, the wide discretion granted to defence lawyers, and the difficulty of overturning convictions based on tactical errors or omissions. The chapter concludes by discussing forensic misconduct and the systemic issues within forensic institutions.

Police Conduct

In the previous chapter, we considered the risk of bias and tunnel vision in police decision-making. As in other international research (e.g. Covey, 2012; Eady, 2009; Hoyle, 2023), there is also a close association between police misconduct and wrongful convictions in Australia, a relationship often evidenced by inquiries into police misconduct and investigations by police oversight bodies. These include the Royal Commission into the Management of Police Informants in Victoria (2020), the Queensland Commission of Inquiry into Possible Illegal Activities and Associated Police Misconduct (1989) ("Fitzgerald Inquiry"), Royal Commission in the NSW Police Service (1997) ("Wood Commission"), Board of Inquiry into Allegations against members of Victoria Police Force (1976) ("Beach Inquiry"), Committee of Inquiry into the enforcement of criminal law in Queensland (1977) ("Lucas Inquiry"), and NSW Royal Commission of Inquiry into Drug trafficking (1983) ("Stewart Royal Commission").

The practice of police giving false evidence of a confession, known as 'verballing', for example, was rife in Australia from the 1980s to early 2000s (Alderson, 2001, p. 263). Other police misconduct includes evidence tampering and non-disclosure (Ruyters et al., 2021). Andrew Mallard's case is a well-known example of several forms of police misconduct. In 1995, Mallard was wrongfully convicted of murdering Pamela Lawrence. No forensic evidence linked Mallard with the crime scene, and his conviction relied heavily on a series of admissions obtained during police interviews, most of which were unrecorded and documented solely in police notes (Crime and Misconduct Commission, 2008). Crucially, the police conducted tests demonstrating that a wrench, which Mallard allegedly confessed to using, could not have caused the victim's injuries. This evidence was shared with the prosecution but never disclosed to the defence or the court (Crime and Misconduct Commission, 2008, p. 103; *Mallard v the Queen* ("*Mallard*") (2005) 224 CLR 125 [56]). The police also tampered with forensic reports and altered key witness statements to reinforce the case against Mallard, again without disclosing these manipulations (Crime and Misconduct Commission, 2008, p. xxvi–xxv; *Mallard*, [56]). The undisclosed material was uncovered several years later, and Mallard was released after the Director of Public Prosecutions discontinued the case. A Cold Case Review later identified a new suspect based on fresh forensic evidence (Crime and Misconduct Commission, 2008).

Another example of evidence tampering occurred in the case of Jason Roberts. With his co-accused Bandali Debs, Jason Roberts was convicted of the 1998 shooting murders of the two police officers. One officer made a dying declaration referring to the two offenders, which became critical in the subsequent investigation and case against Roberts. He unsuccessfully appealed against his conviction and was refused special leave to appeal to the High Court (*Roberts v The Queen* [2020] VSCA 277,[4]). Roberts lodged three petitions of mercy claiming that he was not present during the murders. His statements were supported by alibi evidence and material obtained through an investigation by the Independent Broad-based Anti-Corruption Commission (IBAC), which cast doubt on whether the dying officer had referred to two offenders. The Commission found serious disclosure obligation failures and improper practices by police, including omitting relevant information from witness statements, officers making mutually collaborative statements, and disposal of signed statements (IBAC, 2020, p. 11). The Court of Appeal quashed his convictions, and Roberts was subsequently acquitted on retrial (*Roberts v The Queen* [2020] VSCA 277).

Police Culture

The problem of police culture (Ruyters et al., 2021) is a recurring theme in various commissions and inquiries into police conduct. Corruption in policing is often linked to the area of enforcement in which officers work, with specialist squads being particularly vulnerable due to their frequent exposure to criminal actors and incentives for misconduct (Bleakley, 2019). In 2020, the Victorian Royal Commission into the Management of Police Informants reported on the investigation of the use of the barrister Nicola Gobbo as a police informant handled through a Source Development Unit (SDU). Gobbo secretly provided information about her own clients through her handlers to the Purana Task Force, a specialist unit established to respond to escalating gangland violence between organised crime groups. Gobbo's conduct violated legal professional privilege and compromised the convictions of more than 1011 people (RCMPI, Final Report Summary, 2020, p. 17). The Commission found evidence of systemic failure marked by a police culture focused on results at any cost, poor ethical decision-making, disregard for human rights, and resistance to accountability and transparency (RCMPI, 2020, p. 205). The Commission report highlighted severe deficiencies in oversight and ethical conduct within the Victoria Police.

The result focus of police is also implicated in the cultivation of informer witnesses and the use of covert strategies to elicit confessions, such as the Mr. Big Technique, and in the reliance on credibility assessments through polygraphs and content analysis rather than investigating alternatives. These issues are discussed in Chap. 11.

The Conduct of the Prosecution

While police misconduct is often the first point of failure in wrongful conviction cases, the role of prosecutors is equally critical. Recognised as one of six 'canonical' factors underlying wrongful convictions in the United States, prosecutor misconduct is frequently cited as a cause for wrongful convictions (Jochnowitz & Kendall, 2021; Joy, 2006) with a report by the National Registry of Exonerations finding prosecutorial misconduct in 30% of exonerations (National Registry, 2020, p. 12).

Wrongful convictions resulting from prosecutorial misconduct in Australia, however, are rare. We distinguish between misconduct, which we define as conduct determined by a court to be improper, such as in Andrew Mallard's case, and other acts and omissions—including imputed conduct—that might result in a miscarriage of justice but do not meet the threshold of misconduct. Using this definition, for example, we would not include the cases of Douglas Jensen and Emily Perry identified in a 2015 analysis of known wrongful convictions in Australia as instances of wrongful convictions caused by prosecutorial misconduct (Dioso-Villa, 2015). The High Court was critical about the use of similar fact evidence in Emily Perry's case, but there was no finding of misconduct (*Perry v The Queen* ("*Perry*") (1982) 150 CLR 580). There was also no finding of misconduct in Douglas Jensen's case, where the self-represented Jensen was granted an appeal and a new trial on the grounds of the prosecution's failure to call a material witness (*R v Jensen* [2009] VSCA 266).

Prosecutors' duties are set out in Rule 29 of the *Legal Profession Uniform Law Australian Solicitors' Conduct Rules* 2015. These include the duty to fairly assist the court to arrive at the truth, the duty to disclose, the duty not to bias the court against the accused, and the duty not to argue a proposition which the prosecutor does not believe on reasonable grounds to be capable of contributing to a finding of guilt. Groundless prosecutions may result in civil action for malicious prosecutions (e.g. *Wood v State of New South Wales* [2018] NSWSC 1247). Failures to comply with these duties can result in miscarriages of justice but are not necessarily misconduct. For instance, the decision not to call a witness, such as in Douglas Jensen's case, may be an error in judgement (*The Queen v Apostilides* (1984) 154 CLR 563, p. 575; but see *Gilham v The Queen* below), and there are also several circumstances in which the prosecution does not need to call a witness (see, e.g. *Whitehorn v The Queen* (1983) 152 CLR 657). There are, however, clear dangers in relying on prosecution case theories in weak circumstantial cases.

In *Gilham v The Queen* [2012] NSWCCA 131, the NSW Court of Criminal Appeal was critical of prosecution conduct, which also included inflammatory and inappropriate words and manner by the Crown Prosecutor in cross-examination of the defendant and in her closing address ([433]). The Court found that the prosecutor's failure to call an expert witness who held a different opinion from other prosecution witnesses, and which contradicted the Crown case theory, constituted a miscarriage of justice ([404], [412]). Gilham had two trials. In the first trial, the Crown prosecutor had rejected the expert report, which had been requested by the prosecution, as "plainly unreliable" ([270]). That assessment of the report was "uncritically adopted" by the prosecutor in the second trial ([394]). The Court stopped short of finding misconduct but noted at [670]:

> Even were the new evidence ground as it concerns the issue of carbon monoxide not successful, the appeal would have been upheld on other grounds,

> including one at least that involved a finding of prosecutorial misconduct in the marshalling of the evidence to support the proposition that there was a pattern in the similarity in the knife wounds - a circumstance used by the Crown as the central motif in its case before the jury.

In *Anderson v The Queen* (1991) 53 A Crim R 421, the failure to recall a witness by the same Crown prosecutor from Gilham's first trial was found to be unfair. Anderson's trial was miscarried largely because of the prosecution's failure to check a case theory, which was compounded by an 'inappropriate and unfair attempt by the Crown Prosecutor to persuade the jury to draw inferences of fact which were not open on the evidence' (p. 453).

The Crown prosecutor who appeared in Gilham's first trial and in Anderson's trial was also criticised by the New South Wales Court of Criminal Appeal in *Wood v The Queen* [2012] NSWCCA 21 for using impermissible reasoning [294], innuendo [305], and fiction [335]. Gordon Wood had successfully appealed his 2008 murder conviction on the grounds that included prejudice by the Crown Prosecutor. The Court of Criminal Appeal found that asking the jury to consider whether Wood provided satisfactory answers to 50 rhetorical questions posed by the prosecutor in his final address reversed the onus of proof and was an 'impermissible course' for the prosecutor to follow ([605]). Wood unsuccessfully sued the State of New South Wales for malicious prosecution (*Wood v State of New South Wales* [2018] NSWSC 1247). Fullerton J did not find the necessary malice despite the prosecutor's 'demonstrable failures' of forensic judgement and despite grave suspicions that some of the prosecutor's closing submissions 'might have been a deliberate attempt by him to unfairly influence the jury, or even to deliberately prejudice the plaintiff by the patently and grossly improper technique of utilising smear, innuendo or speculation' [1344].

Prosecutorial misconduct is sometimes conflated in reports with other official misconduct (e.g. National Registry, 2020). This may be due to the essential relationship between police and prosecution, which results, for instance, in imputing knowledge of disclosable materials held by police, about which they may not be aware (Guerrieri, 2000; *Visser v DPP* [2020] VSCA 327 [77]). It is important, however, to make a distinction between actions by the police and prosecution and isolate the conduct that might initiate an error leading to a wrongful conviction. For instance, in *R v Grey* (2001) 75 ALJR 1708, the prosecution's failure to disclose a "letter of comfort" provided by police to a key prosecution witness resulted in a miscarriage of justice and an order for a new trial. The prosecutor was unaware of the existence of the letter but conceded in the Court of Appeal and the High Court that this failure was a breach of the prosecution's duty to disclose (*R v Grey* (2001) 75 ALJR 1708 [30]).

More recently, in the well-known case of Lawyer X, the High Court held that Victoria Police's use and encouragement of a lawyer to provide information about her own clients corrupted the prosecution of each accused 'in a manner which debased fundamental premises of the criminal justice system' (*AB (a pseudonym) v CD (a pseudonym)* [2018] HCA 58[10]. This information was not disclosed to the Director of Public Prosecutions, and consequently, there was no opportunity for the prosecution to take remedial action, such as withdrawing the prosecutions (RCMPI, 2020, p. 5). As a consequence of a Royal Commission into the Management of Police Informants, disclosure practices have been amended in Victoria to introduce disclosure certificates to remind the police of their disclosure obligations to the prosecution (RCMPI, ch. 14, 2020). The prevalence of non-disclosure practices is further discussed in Chap. 5.

Conduct of the Defence

Trial lawyers have a responsibility to 'make tactical decisions and assess risks' (*TKWJ v The Queen* "TKWJ" (2002) 212 CLR 124, p. 131, Gleeson CJ). There is a risk of wrongful conviction through defence lawyers' wide discretion at trial because their decision-making in proceedings ("forensic decision-making") is rarely reviewable. Defendants are bound by their lawyer's conduct even if they disagree with decisions their lawyer makes in conducting their defence (*R v Birks* "Birks" (1990) 19 NSWLR 677, pp. 683, 685; *TKWJ,* 2002), including whether they testify at their trial. Holding a defendant to tactical decisions made by their lawyer at trial will not, in itself, amount to a miscarriage of justice, even if the decisions are made without or contrary to the defendant's instructions (*Ratten v The Queen* (1974) 131 CLR 510, p. 517; *Slater v The Queen* [2020] VSCA 270; *Huggins v The State of Western Australia* [2018] WASC 61, [2]). These decisions effectively result in defendants being silenced in their own proceedings. These decisions can result in the loss of critical opportunities to question and call witnesses, which cannot generally be corrected by an appeal.

Circumstances in which forensic decision-making has not amounted to a miscarriage of justice include, e.g., failing to seek an anti-tendency direction (*Hamilton (a pseudonym)* 2021 HCA 33), deciding not to call evidence of good character (*TKWJ,* 2002, 'actively resisting' directions (*Kramer v The Queen* [2023] NSWCCA 152), failing to lead available medical evidence (*Lyndon v The Queen* [2014] NSWCCA 112), failing to cross-examine (*Name Suppressed v The King* [2023] NSWCCA 130; *Ali v The Queen* (2005) HCA 8) ("*Ali*"), failing to adduce evidence about the effects of Foetal Alcohol Spectrum Disorder (*Foster v The King* [2023] NTCCA 5, and failing to object to the reception of evidence (*Ali* [25]). Providing advice to plead guilty in circumstances where innocence is later established is also, of itself, unlikely to amount to a miscarriage of justice. False guilty pleas are discussed further in this book.

Allegations of incompetent defence are common in wrongful conviction claims and in applications we receive at the Innocence Initiative (Drummond & Mills, 2020; Green, 2012). In considering whether a lawyer's conduct amounts to a miscarriage of justice, the court first determines whether the act or omission resulted in a material irregularity in the trial in the light of their wide discretion 'to conduct the trial as he or she thinks best' (*TKWJ,* 2002, p. 149, McHugh J). The court then considers whether there is a 'significant possibility that the irregularity deprived the defendant on a chance of acquittal that was fairly open' (*TKWJ*, 2002, p. 133, Gaudron J; p.149, McHugh J). Any error by the defence lawyer that resulted in a miscarriage of justice will lead to an appeal (*Ignjatic (1993)* 68 A Crim R 333; *TKWJ*, 2002, p. 150, McHugh J) but appeals based on allegations of a lawyer's incompetence must show that the miscarriage of justice was caused by the incompetence, which may be difficult to establish (*TKWJ,* 2002, pp. 147, 149, McHugh J).

A lawyer's 'flagrant incompetence' may, however, give rise to a miscarriage of justice (*Nudd v The Queen* "Nudd" [2006] HCA 9; *Kamali v The Queen* [2019] NSWCCA 186 [31], as may a combination of events including their incompetence (*R v Birks* (1990) 19 NSWLR 677; *D'Orta-Ekenaike v Victoria Legal Aid* (2005) 223 CLR 1, p. 64, McHugh J). In *R v Birks* (1990) 19 NSWLR 677, the Court of Appeal found that the defence lawyer's failure to cross-examine a complainant in accordance with instructions and subsequent failure to correct the omission was 'flagrant incompetence' resulting in a miscarriage of justice. The success of this ground for appeal is likely to depend on the strength of the prosecution case. In *Nudd,* where the defence lawyer's incompetence included failing to obtain Nudd's version of events at any time and misunderstanding the elements of the offence in question, the High Court dismissed the appeal regarding the prosecution case as 'effectively unanswerable' [*Nudd,* 2006, [104], Kirby J [159]–[160], Callinan and Heydon JJ).

As McHugh J pointed out in *TKWJ,* however, '[n]ot every error makes the trial unfair (p. 148). In the same case, Gleeson CJ was clear that while the trial lawyer's decisions about the calling of evidence might later be regretted, this did not 'make the client a victim of unfairness' (p. 131). Forensic choices that other competent lawyers might have made, for instance, are not likely to be enough to establish that a miscarriage has occurred (*TKWJ,* 2002, p. 150, McHugh; *Ignjatic* (1993) 68 A Crim R 333; *Hamilton (a pseudonym)* 2021 HCA 33 [49), nor will reasonable explanations for any act or omission (e.g., *TKWJ,* 2002, p. 131, Gaudron J; pp159–160, Hayne J), which potentially includes lack of preparation time.

Other decision-making may be out of the defence lawyer's control. For example, it is common for the evidence of one agency or group to be given through a single witness, which is often justified on an efficiency of resource basis. So, only one emergency services officer might testify even though several attended the crime scene and subsequently made statements. Police evidence is often given through a single representative of the unit, so if 14 police attended a crime scene, only half of that number might make a statement, and only two or four might give evidence on behalf of several. This funnelling effect means that there is no certainty in most cases that the crime scene narrative presented at trial is the actual crime scene that confronted police and crime scene investigators. The defence have also lost or conceded an opportunity to question other police about matters that only they observed. As we argue further in this book, inadequate legal assistance also poses a critical risk, often preventing defence lawyers from conducting thorough investigations or preparing adequately for trial. Limited resources constrain their ability to explore alternative defence strategies, address complex evidence, or effectively handle growing demands in an increasingly underfunded legal assistance sector.

Forensic Misconduct

Forensic misconduct refers to corruption, fraud, or other misconduct by forensic scientists and experts, most commonly in favour of the prosecution (Giannelli, 1997, 2007; Turvey, 2013). Misconduct includes fabricating of data, falsification of results and credentials, and plagiarism (Turvey, 2013). Forensic fraud occurs when forensic experts provide sworn testimony, opinions, or documents that contain deceptive or misleading findings, opinions, or conclusions, deliberately offered to secure an unfair or unlawful gain (Turvey, 2013). The topic of forensic misconduct is prominent in the US literature, as most crime laboratories in the United States are administered by law enforcement agencies where there are inherent structural incentives to favour prosecution (Giannelli, 1997; Peterson et al., 1985; Jonakait, 1991; Moenssens, 1993; Turvey, 2013). Unlike in the United States, forensic laboratories in Australia are in a variety of government agencies, including law enforcement, health, justice, and science agencies (Wilson-Wilde et al., 2019). While this would appear to lower the risk of structural pressures leading to misconduct, this independence may not eliminate the risk of pro-prosecution bias among forensic experts (Findley & Scott, 2006). Jeanguenat and Dror (2018) noted that human factors, such as workplace stress and anxiety, and work volume can also affect the quality of forensic decision-making.

In Australia, wrongful convictions appear more likely to result from error or misplaced managerialism than misconduct, as forensic science processes have appeared as a key risk factor for wrongful convictions. A 2022 Commission of Inquiry ("Sofronoff Inquiry") into forensic DNA testing at Queensland Health Forensic and Scientific Services (QHFSS), Queensland's main forensic laboratory, found that testing thresholds were changed in 2018 to increase efficiency and save cost (Sofronoff, 2022, p. 266 [831]). This led to samples with low levels being reported as having no detectable DNA or insufficient DNA for processing (Sofronoff, 2022, p. 40 [187]). Consequently, many samples were not tested, and others were deemed to contain insufficient DNA for further testing. The inquiry had been instigated after the popularity of a podcast by *The Australian*'s Hedley Thomas into the murder of Shandee Blackburn. The podcast raised serious doubts regarding the testing of biological material found at the crime scene, which failed to return a positive result for DNA (Sofronoff, 2022, p. iv). The inquiry found mismanagement, dishonesty, and ineffective work culture and made 123 recommendations to improve processes at QHFSS (Sofronoff, 2022, p. xii). A subsequent inquiry made further recommendations, and both inquiries have led to the mass retesting of previously disregarded samples (Bennett, 2023).

Alan Staines is another example of forensic misconduct. Staines was convicted of burglary in 2005 and received a suspended sentence. Staines had pleaded guilty on the advice of his lawyer as his DNA was a match to DNA obtained from a blood stain left at the crime scene (*Staines v West* [2017] WASC 330 [1–[2]). The sample had been tested at the state pathology service PathWest Laboratory Medicine WA. In 2016, PathWest discovered an error; the match was to another person who had the same first name and surname (*Staines v West* [2017] WASC 330 [3]; Public Sector Commission, 2017, p. 5). His conviction was quashed on appeal and followed by an inquiry to determine whether misconduct by PathWest staff had compromised evidence, results, or reports to Western Australia Police or the Office of the Director of Public Prosecutions (Ross, 2017, p. 1). The Inquiry examined 19 cases involving 27 persons of interest, which had been identified by the ODPP as potentially compromised and found 11 anomalous results. The report noted several deficiencies in processes, including the use of outdated technology and systems, poor governance, the risk of contextual and confirmation bias, and a reliance on manual processes when better systems were available (Ross, 2017).

Discussions about forensic misconduct leading to wrongful convictions in Australia have largely been focused on one individual, Dr. Colin Manock, who was the chief forensic pathologist for South Australia for many years despite a lack of qualifications (ABC Radio National, 2022). Manock is associated with over 400 criminal convictions (ABC Radio Adelaide, 2015; Moles, 2015) and his evidence, later established as incorrect, directly led to the wrongful conviction of Henry Keogh (*R v Keogh (No 2)* ("*Keogh*") [2014] SASCFC 136). Henry Keogh was convicted in 1995 of murdering his fiancée, Anna-Jane Cheney, who was found drowned in a bathtub in their Adelaide home. The conviction relied heavily on Manock's testimony that Cheney's death was not accidental, suggesting that Keogh had forcibly drowned her by holding her leg based on the presence of apparent bruises on her legs (*Keogh,* 2014, [154]). After the trial, Manock recanted significant parts of his evidence and acknowledged that his conclusions about bruising were wrong (*Keogh,* 2014, [16], [154]). Keogh's first appeal was dismissed but appealed again in 2014 following the enactment of the 353A *Criminal Law Consolidation Act 1935* (SA), which introduced second or subsequent appeal provisions. Amongst other evidence, two independent forensic pathologists considered Manock's autopsy to be "inadequate in material respects" and agreed the medical evidence did not suggest the death was a homicide or discount the death being accidental (*Keogh* 2014, [22], [23]). Keogh's conviction was quashed and he was released from prison after serving for nearly

20 years. This case raised serious concerns about the standards of forensic evidence in South Australia and led to a broader scrutiny of Dr. Manock's role in other criminal cases (Moles, 2015).

Legislation

Criminal Law Consolidation Act 1935 (SA)

Cases

AB (a pseudonym) v CD (a pseudonym) [2018] HCA 58
Ali v The Queen (2005) HCA 8
Anderson v The Queen (1991) 53 A Crim R 421
D'Orta-Ekenaike v Victoria Legal Aid (2005) 223 CLR 1
Foster v The King [2023] NTCCA 5
Gilham v The Queen [2012] NSWCCA 131
Hamilton (a pseudonym) 2021 HCA 33
Huggins v The State of WA [2018] WASCA 61
Ignjatic (1993) 68 A Crim R 333
Kamali v The Queen [2019] NSWCCA 186
Kramer v The Queen [2023] NSWCCA 152)
Lyndon v The Queen [2014] NSWCCA 112)
Mickelberg v The Queen [2004] WASCA 145
(*Name Suppressed v The King* [2023] NSWCCA 130
Nudd v The Queen (2006) 162 A Crim R 301
Perry v The Queen (1982) 150 CLR 580
R v Birks (1990) 19 NSWLR 677
R v Grey (2001) 75 ALJR 1708
R v Jensen [2009] VSCA 266
R v Keogh (No 2) [2014] SASCFC 136
R v Mallard (2005) 224 CLR 125
Ratten v The Queen (1974) 131 CLR 510
Roberts v The Queen [2020] VSCA 277
Slater v The Queen [2020] VSCA 270
Staines v West [2017] WASC 330
The Queen v Apostilides (1984) 154 CLR 563
TKWJ v The Queen (2002) 212 CLR 124
Visser v DPP [2020] VSCA 327
Whitehorn v The Queen (1983) 152 CLR 657
Wood v State of New South Wales [2018] NSWSC 1247

References

ABC Radio Adelaide. (2015, 21/07/2015). *Flawed murder conviction ruling prompts forensic evidence doubts in other SA murder cases.* https://www.abc.net.au/news/2015-07-21/flawed-murder-convictions-forensic-evidence-other-appeals/6636126

ABC Radio National. (2022). *The case of the underqualified forensic pathologist.* Retrieved 07/11/2024 from https://www.abc.net.au/listen/programs/latenightlive/the-case-of-the-underqualified-forensic-pathologist/13748792

Alderson, K. (2001). *Powers and responsibilities: Reforming NSW criminal investigation law* UNSW Sydney].

Bennett, A. (2023). *Final report: Commission of Inquiry to examine DNA project 13 concerns.* https://www.dnaproject13inquiry.qld.gov.au/assets/DNA%20Project%2013%20Report.pdf.

Bleakley, P. (2019). Watching the watchers: Taskforce Argos and the evidentiary issues involved with infiltrating Dark Web child exploitation networks. *The Police Journal, 92*(3), 221–236.

Covey, R. (2012). Police misconduct as a cause of wrongful convictions. *Washington University Law Review, 90*, 1133.

Corruption and Crime Commission. (2008). *Report on the Inquiry Into Alleged Misconduct by Public Officers in Connection with the Investigation of the Murder of Mrs Pamela Lawrence, the Prosecution and Appeals of Mr Andrew Mark Mallard, and Other Related Matters.* C. a. C. Commission. ccc.wa.gov.au/node/637

Dioso-Villa, R. (2015). A repository of wrongful convictions in Australia: First steps toward estimating prevalence and causal contributing factors. *Flinders Law Journal, 17*(2), 163–202.

Drummond, C. B., & Mills, M. N. (2020). Addressing official misconduct: Increasing accountability in reducing wrongful convictions. *Wrongful Conviction Law Review, 1*, 270.

Eady, D. (2009). *Miscarriages of justice: The uncertainty principle.* Cardiff University (United Kingdom).

Findley, K. A., & Scott, M. S. (2006). Multiple dimensions of tunnel vision in criminal cases. *The Wisconsin Law Review, 291.*

Giannelli, P. C. (1997). The abuse of scientific evidence in criminal cases: The need for independent crime laboratories. *Virginia Journal of Social Policy & the Law, 4*, 439–478.

Giannelli, P. C. (2007). Wrongful convictions and forensic science: The need to regulate crime labs. *North Carolina Law Review, 86*, 163–235.

Green, A. (2012). Challenging the refusal to investigate evidence neglected by trial lawyers. In *The criminal cases review commission* (pp. 46–58). Springer.

Guerrieri, F. F. (2000). Law & (and) order: Redefining the relationship between prosecutors and police. *S. Ill. ULJ, 25*, 353.

Hoyle, C. (2023). Review of wrongful convictions following police misconduct: A study of the English criminal cases review commission. *Monatsschrift für Kriminologie und Strafrechtsreform, 106*(3), 214–226.

Independent Broad-based Anti-corruption Commission. (2020). Operation Gloucester – An investigation into improper evidentiary and disclosure practices in relation to the Victoria Police investigation of the murders of Sergeant Gary Silk and Senior Constable Rodney Miller. V. G. Printer. ibac.vic.gov.au/publications-and-resources/article/operation-gloucester-special-report-july-2020

Informants, R. C. i. t. M. o. P. (2020). *Final report*, November 2020. V. G. Printer.

Jeanguenat, A. M., & Dror, I. E. (2018). Human factors effecting forensic decision making: Workplace stress and well-being. *Journal of Forensic Sciences, 63*(1), 258–261.

Jochnowitz, L. D., & Kendall, T. (2021). *Analyzing structural wrongful convictions.*

Jonakait, R. N. (1991). Forensic science: The need for regulation. *Harvard Journal of Law & Technology, 4*, 109–191.

Joy, P. A. (2006). Relationship between prosecutorial misconduct and wrongful convictions: Shaping remedies for a broken system. *The Wisconsin Law Review, 399.*

Moenssens, A. A. (1993). Novel scientific evidence in criminal cases: Some words of caution. *Journal of Criminal Law & Criminology, 84*, 1–21.

Moles, R. (2015). Institutional reform in the context of criminal appeals in South Australia. *Flinders Law Journal, 17*(2), 331–380.

National Registry of Exonerations. (2020). *Government misconduct and convicting the innocent: The role of prosecutors, police and other law enforcement.* National Registry of Exonerations. Retrieved 07/11/2024 from https://www.law.umich.edu/special/exoneration/Documents/Government_Misconduct_and_Convicting_the_Innocent.pdf

Peterson, J. L., Mihajlovic, S., & Bedrosian, J. L. (1985). The capabilities, uses, and effects of the nation's criminalistics laboratories. *Journal of Forensic Sciences, 30*(1), 10–23. https://doi.org/10.1520/JFS10959J

Public Sector Commission. (2017). *Review of the PathWest forensic biology department.* https://www.parliament.wa.gov.au/publications/tabledpapers.nsf/displaypaper/4010966a294abcea0b147892482581e00007fe39/$file/966.pdf

Ross, A. (2017). *Ross inquiry into PathWest laboratory medicine WA*. D. o. H. Government of Western Australia. https://www.health.wa.gov.au/~/media/Files/Corporate/Reports-and-publications/PathWest/PathWest-Inquiry.pdf

Royal Commission into the Management of Police Informants. (2020). *Chapter 14: Use and disclosure of information from human sources in criminal prosecutions.* Retrieved 07/11/2024 from https://rcmpi.vic.gov.au/volume-iv-landing-page/chapter-14

Ruyters, M., Stratton, G., & Bartle, J. (2021). The culture of non-disclosure and miscarriages of justice. *Alternative Law Journal, 46*(4), 299–306.

Sofronoff, W. (2022). *Final report: Commission of Inquiry into forensic DNA testing in Queensland.* https://www.health.qld.gov.au/__data/assets/pdf_file/0036/1196685/final-report-coi-dna-testing-qld-dec-2022.pdf

Turvey, B. E. (2013). *Forensic fraud: Evaluating law enforcement and forensic science cultures in the context of examiner misconduct.*

Wilson-Wilde, L., Romano, H., & Smith, S. (2019). Error rates in proficiency testing in Australia. *Australian Journal of Forensic Sciences, 51*(sup1), S268–S271.

CHAPTER 5

Practice in the System: The Management of Evidence

Abstract This chapter examines the cultural and institutional practices associated with the management of evidence through the criminal justice system that contribute to error. While forensic error is often assumed to be a central cause of miscarriages of justice, Australian cases frequently reveal more complex systemic issues, which are deeply rooted in investigative culture, evidence management, and disclosure practices. This chapter explores how informal investigative norms, such as reliance on intuition, tunnel vision, and resource-driven shortcuts, interact with flawed forensic processes, disclosure failures, and inadequate evidence preservation to create error. In particular, we emphasise how cultural attitudes within police shape the interpretation, handling, disclosure, and preservation of evidence. Existing standards and conditions for evidence storage also raise concerns about the availability of crucial material for post-conviction review. This chapter emphasises the need for rigorous standards, proper training, and oversight to mitigate these risks and prevent wrongful convictions.

Keywords Wrongful conviction • Evidence management • Investigative errors • Non-disclosure • Forensic error • Evidence preservation

M. Ruyters et al., *Innocence Unveiled*,
https://doi.org/10.1007/978-3-031-91343-3_5

Surprising perhaps for those familiar with the literature on wrongful convictions, very few of the cases that we and other Australian innocence projects investigate have turned on forensic error. Similarly, relatively few well-known wrongful conviction cases have been cited in Australian research as resulting from forensic error or misconduct in Australia (Smith & Urbas, 2019, p. 73), although research in 2015 found that forensic error or misleading forensic evidence was a significant causal and contributing factor in wrongful convictions (Dioso-Villa, 2015, p. 182). The rape conviction cases of Frank Button and Farah Jama are clear examples of this. In Button's case, post-conviction DNA analysis established that another person had committed the crime, while Jama's innocence was established on re-testing of the DNA evidence (*R v Button* [2001] QCA 133; *R v Jama* [2009] VSCA, *unrep*, 7 December 2009). In other cases, the reliability of expert evidence has been a key factor. For instance, the board of inquiry into David Eastman's conviction was scathing of the partisan evidence given by the gunshot residue expert Barnes (e.g. Eastman Inquiry, 2014, pp. 281, 282), and the South Australian Court of Criminal Appeal found that Dr. Manock's evidence 'materially misled the prosecution, the defence, the trial judge and the jury' (*R v Keogh (no 2)* [2014] SASCFC 136 [353]).

In this chapter, we consider how evidence is managed from the initial crime scene investigation to the preservation of evidence for appeals. We highlight the risks inherent in the management, interpretation, and presentation of evidence, which can contribute to wrongful convictions. These challenges arise not only from forensic errors, witness misidentification, and investigative flaws but also from systemic issues such as disclosure failures and inadequate evidence preservation. Cases such as those of Frank Button and Farah Jama illustrate the devastating consequences when evidence is mishandled and underline the importance of rigorous standards in evidence collection, handling, and analysis, alongside the critical need for proper training and oversight of forensic professionals.

Beyond forensics, investigative errors are recognised as a significant factor in wrongful convictions. Decision-making based on intuition rather than evidence-based processes, tunnel vision, and resource constraints often leads investigators to prematurely narrow their focus on a single suspect, ignoring alternative explanations or potentially exculpatory evidence. Failures by the police and prosecution to disclose evidence have also been repeatedly implicated in miscarriages of justice. Cases such as *Mallard v The Queen* and *Roberts v The Queen* illustrate the systemic barriers faced by defendants in accessing critical evidence, raising questions about the adequacy of the current disclosure frameworks in Australia. The chapter concludes with the essential role of evidence preservation, particularly in the context of post-conviction reviews. Inadequate evidence storage and handling practices, compounded by a lack of national standards, significantly limit post-conviction options.

Management of the Crime Scene

Police investigations are designed to uncover the circumstances of an offence, identify perpetrators, and collect sufficient evidence to support prosecution. Every investigation involves numerous decisions, each carrying the potential for error, which, cumulatively, could contribute to a wrongful conviction. The investigative process has several key stages, beginning with the attendance of first responders to secure the crime scene, prevent evidence contamination, and provide early observations that inform the investigation (Delémont et al., 2017). Crime scene examiners collect physical evidence at the crime scene, such as forensic samples and fingerprints, and take photographs. Investigators then start to build a case by interviewing witnesses, victims, and suspects, and analysing other evidence, such as surveillance footage or phone records. Finally, when sufficient evidence points to a suspect, an arrest is made, and the case moves forward in the prosecution process.

Despite the importance of criminal investigations, research has consistently found that investigators frequently rely on "hunches" and "intuition" rather than formal evidence-based processes in decided the trajectory of an investigation (Akinci & Sadler-Smith, 2020; Boulton & Cole, 2016; Cordner & Scott, 2014, p. 3588). This is sometimes euphemistically referred to as utilising 'professional judgment' to make strategic decisions regarding the course of an investigation (Leach, 2023, p. 71). Our experience in investigating wrongful convictions suggests that errors can occur as a result of this kind of decision-making by investigators, including narrowing in on a single suspect while overlooking alternative suspects or potentially exculpatory evidence, failing to collect the best available evidence, and failing to exhaust all possible leads related to an investigation, often justified based on resource limitations.

Effective processing of a crime scene is crucial in police investigations (Kelty et al., 2011). In Australia, crime scene examinations are conducted by specialised units within the police trained in crime scene examination and evidence collection (e.g. Victoria Police, 2024). However, the initial securing of crime scenes may be conducted by generalist frontline police officers. Errors can begin early in crime scene examinations because of a poorly secured scene, leading to the loss of evidence or cross-contamination of evidence by third-party sources. A 2017 Report by the New South Wales Police Integrity Commission found that 58% of critical incident scenes in cases involving serious injury or death had been properly preserved over a three-year period meaning that 'potentially 42% of incident scenes were at risk of loss of evidence or interference with evidence through either inadvertence or deliberate misconduct' (Police Integrity Commission, 2017, p. XII).

Despite established protocols aimed at preserving the integrity of crime scene evidence, flaws in collection, handling, and transportation can further lead to contamination, mislabelling, or mishandling of evidence (Alketbi, 2024; Julian et al., 2012). These additional errors can lead to inaccurate or misleading results in any subsequent forensic comparisons and analyses of the collected evidence. Case theories and confirmation bias may also influence how police interpret crime scene evidence, leading them to favour collecting evidence that aligns with pre-existing expectations while overlooking potentially exculpatory evidence at the crime scene (van den Eeden et al., 2016, 2018, p. 110). The devastating impact of failures in evidence handling was illustrated in Farah Jama's case (Vincent, 2010, p. 13).

Mishandling of Evidence

Farah Abdulkadir Jama was wrongfully convicted of rape in 2008 in the County Court of Victoria and sentenced to six years in prison, with a non-parole period of four years. Jama was imprisoned for 15 months before his conviction was set aside by the Victorian Court of Appeal and a verdict of acquittal entered (*R v Jama* [2009] VSCA, *unrep,* 7 December 2009). The prosecution's case, based on a single DNA sample taken from the complainant, was that Jama had raped 48-year-old 'M' in a suburban nightclub. M was found unconscious in a locked toilet cubicle and had no memory of the event. Fearing that she had been sexually assaulted, M presented at a crisis care unit, where she was examined by a doctor who took vaginal swabs for analysis. Coincidentally, the same doctor had taken forensic samples 28 hours previously from another woman 'B' who had been engaged in sexual activity with Jama. No charges had been filed in this case (Vincent, 2010, p. 13). A subsequent inquiry found that the seminal deposit on B's hair had been transferred to the sample taken from M at some point during M's medical examination (Vincent, 2010, p. 58). The Office of Public Prosecutions accepted that there had been a miscarriage of justice after investigating the potential link between B and M's cases and the possibility of contamination while preparing for Jama's appeal (Vincent, 2010, pp. 46–47).

Questions had been raised shortly after Jama's conviction about the strength of the prosecution case against him and the reliability of the DNA evidence. Crucially, other than the DNA evidence, there was no evidence to suggest that M had been assaulted in the nightclub. Jama had an alibi for the period in which the assault was said to have occurred nor was there any CCTV footage of Jama at the nightclub. Despite these concerns being raised early in the police investigation by at least one police officer involved in the case, senior investigators decided to pursue the case anyway.

Non-disclosure of Evidence

Well-documented non-disclosure practices in Australia present a continuing risk of wrongful convictions. Prosecutors have a duty to disclose all relevant material to the defence, including evidence that might weaken the prosecution's case or support the defence (*Grey v the Queen* "Grey" (2001) 75 ALJR 1708; *Mallard v The Queen* "Mallard" (2005) 224 CLR 125, p. 150, Kirby J). This obligation extends to material that the prosecution does not intend to use (*Mallard,* 2005). The duty, which is subject to any claims of public interest immunity, legal professional privilege, or contrary statutory provision, is found in common law, statutes, and prosecutorial guidelines (e.g. Criminal Procedure Act 2009 (Vic) Parts 4.4 and 5.5; Legal Profession Uniform Conduct (Barristers) Rules 2015; Commonwealth Director of Public Prosecutions "CDPP", 2017). The duty is owed to the court (*Roberts v The Queen* "Roberts" [2020] VSCA 58 [56]); *Cannon v Tahche* (2002) VR 317, 340–341), but the defendant's *right* to disclosure arises from the right to a fair trial. Non-disclosure deprives the defendant of material that might assist their defence and deprives them of the opportunity to seek any appropriate remedy for the non-disclosure, such as applying for a stay of the proceedings. Disclosure is an ongoing duty (e.g. *Criminal Procedure Act 2009* (Vic) s 185), and any post-conviction disclosure of unused material by the prosecution could result in a miscarriage of justice and the conviction being set aside (*Mallard,* 2005, p. 156, Kirby J).

The police also have a general duty to disclose all relevant material to the prosecution (*DPP v Galloway (A Pseudonym) and Others* [2014] VSCA 272) (Maxwell P, Neave and Coghlan JJA) and the ability of the prosecution to meet disclosure obligations will usually depend on the extent to which police have complied with their own duty (*R v Ernst* [2020] QCA 150 [35], Sofronoff P and Mullins JA and Davis J). Prosecutors, however, must accept responsibility for deliberate acts by the police to withhold disclosable evidence because the police and prosecution are regarded as part of the same prosecution apparatus for the purposes of disclosure (*Mallard v The Queen* (2005) 224 CLR 125, 132–133; *R v Farquharson* (2009) 26 VR 410, 464, Warren CJ, Nettle and Redlich JJA). This is because, while the prosecution might not have been aware of the breach of the duty to disclose, the whole prosecution apparatus will have failed its disclosure duty (Plater & De Vreeze, 2012, p. 141). This means that the prosecution must be proactive in making enquiries of the police to ensure disclosure obligations have been met, as the defence should not be placed in the position of needing to 'fossick' for information (*Mallard,* p.133, 150–151; *Grey,* 2001, p. 1713; *Anile v The Queen* [2018] VSCA 235 [130] (Priest, Beach and Weinberg JJA). Failing to comply with disclosure obligations through mistake, oversight, or ignorance of the existence of the material, however, is not necessarily misconduct.

As we pointed out under the topic Prosecution Conduct, prosecutorial misconduct is also sometimes conflated in reporting with other forms of official misconduct, including police misconduct (National Registry of Exonerations, 2020; The National Registry of Exonerations, 2024). Much of the non-disclosure dialogue in the United States is addressed under official misconduct, particularly in relation to the prosecution. We want to make a clear distinction between the actions of different officials in the criminal justice system, especially between the prosecution and the police, to isolate the individual culture, practice, and conduct that may trigger or escalate the cascade of errors leading to a wrongful conviction.

The responsibility for disclosure breaches also appears to differ between the United States and Australia. Gould et al. 's study of Brady violations, for example, revealed that prosecutors were solely responsible for 60% of disclosure errors and that at least one-third of non-disclosure was intentional (Gould et al., 2021, pp. 1065, 1082). While there is currently no comparable Australian data, the intentional non-disclosure of evidence by police is more closely linked to miscarriages of justice in Australia (e.g. *Mallard,* 2005; *Orman v The Queen* (2019) 59 VR 511; *Roberts,* 2020). Not all these cases have involved innocence, but they do reveal a cultural propensity in police to resist full disclosure of evidence, a propensity which is well documented in Australia and the United Kingdom (Justice Committee, 2018; McMurdo, 2020; Polykarpou, 2022; Ruyters et al., 2021).

Non-disclosure, late disclosure, and partial disclosure continue to be a problem in Australia. The Royal Commission into the Management of Police Informants in Victoria observed in Victoria Police signs of a culture where police officers are driven to get results at any cost' and 'a culture of exceptionalism; that is, an attitude that police are "special" and can operate outside of rules and policies because of the nature of their work' (McMurdo, 2020, p. 205). While miscarriages of justice can be procedural and substantive (*Roberts v The Queen* [2020] VSCA 277 [33–34]), non-disclosure does not necessarily demonstrate the substantial miscarriage of justice required for criminal appeals in Australia. The appeal court will need to be satisfied that the non-disclosure would have made a difference to the outcome of the trial or undermined the fairness of the trial (*Roberts v The Queen* [2020] VSCA 277). In many cases, establishing the non-disclosure breach may be dependent on the availability of the evidence in question.

Several Australian jurisdictions impose obligations on the police to make a disclosure to the prosecution (NSW, VIC, SA, QLD). For instance, section 110A *Criminal Procedure Act 2009* (Vic), which was introduced in the wake of the Royal Commission to encourage better disclosure by police to the prosecution, provides that police must complete a disclosure certificate describing any material not contained in the police brief which is subject to a claim of privilege or public interest immunity, or a statutory immunity, prohibition, or restriction. The new s415A *Criminal Procedure Act 2009* (Vic) creates an obligation on the informant to disclose to the Director of Public Prosecutions any material that is 'relevant to the alleged offence' other than material subject to a claim of privilege or immunity or statutory prohibition or restriction. The informant must also notify the DPP about the existence and nature of any material that is relevant to the offence and any privilege, immunity, prohibition, or restriction to which the material is subject.

While it is still too early to assess whether there has been an improvement in disclosure processes from police to prosecution in certificate jurisdictions, how these provisions will incentivise police to provide more complete disclosure is unclear. The requirement to disclose material that is relevant to the guilt or innocence of the defendant requires police and prosecution to make an appraisal of the material's relevance to those matters. There is a significant risk, however, that, despite the emphasis on improved disclosure processes, police will continue to assess 'relevance' based on the case they want to bring to trial. Defendants may also be unaware that certain evidence was available to them, potentially due to their lawyers lacking the necessary funding, time, and resources to identify disclosure errors. However, arguments that defence lawyers lacked sufficient time to prepare or detect such errors are unlikely to be accepted as grounds for an appeal.

Preservation of Evidence

The last part of this chapter considers the processes for preserving and managing evidence, which is a crucial part of the criminal justice system. The lack of access to potentially exculpatory evidence, for whatever reason, creates a significant risk that wrongful convictions will remain unremedied. Law enforcement bodies manage vast amounts of property and evidence, including forensic and digital. At all stages, individuals and organisations who manage evidence must ensure that evidence remains secure and has not been contaminated or compromised with an accurate and documented chain of custody. Prosecutions rely on evidence management. Research in the UK found that missing or lost evidence resulted in the collapse of 20,838 Crown Prosecution cases, including 42 homicides, before trial between October 2018 and August 2021 (McCartney & Shorter, 2019, 2023, p. 96). Retention of evidence for post-conviction re-examination is also vital, particularly in cases that rely on new methods or new scientific understandings (Shorter & Madland, 2019, p. 229).

Re-testing of DNA evidence is a significant factor in exonerations in the United States (Strom et al., 2011, p. 134). Many states have evidence-preservation statutes, such as the Post-Conviction Access to Forensic and Scientific Analysis Act introduced in 2012 by the Commonwealth of Massachusetts, which mandates the retention and preservation of evidence in criminal cases. The Act excepts property that might be returned to third parties or property impractical to retain (**§ 16(a)**. Evidence retention policies and legislative frameworks are patchwork, however (National Institute of Standards and Technology (NIST), 2015, p. 8). Similarly, McCartney and Shorter found that UK police forces had '*ad-hoc* in-house policies' for the retention of materials, with many officers unaware of national guidelines on retention periods post-conviction (McCartney & Shorter, 2020, pp. 125, 132). Shorter and Madland (2019, p. 239) described the current police storage in the UK as 'disjointed, inadequately resourced and, at times poorly managed'.

Australian courts have consistently held that the loss of evidence does not necessarily mean an unfair trial (*El Bayeh v The Queen* (2011) 206 A Crim R 541, pp. 552–553 [36]); *Eastman v Director of Public Prosecutions (No.13)* [2016] ACTCA 65 [269]; *R v Smith* [No 1] [2011] NSWSC 725 [80], [92]). However, there are no national standards for managing police property, which raises concerns about the consistency and reliability of evidence handling across jurisdictions (CCC, 2005, p. 12). Property management policies are found in police manuals such as the Victoria Police Manual (VPM) or the Queensland Police Operational Procedures Manual (OPM), and there are varied practices across Australia.

Police property is also usually stored across a wide range of locations, including many that are not appropriate for storage (CCC, 2005, p. 25). In June 2018, for instance, Victoria Police had possession of 470,000 items stored at over 200 locations (VAGO, 2018, p. 7; see also CCC, 2005, p. 25). In Western Australia, property, including exhibits, was found stored in locations which were not designed for that purpose, such as garages, sea containers, cupboards, and even outdoors, often using a range of metal, wood, and plastic crate shelving (CCC, 2005, pp. 25, 26). Here, the Western Australia Police retained custody of exhibits from the point of collection to destruction or return (CCC, 2005, p. 17). While centralised storage facilities are common across jurisdictions, police units also often maintain temporary storage for transit at police stations (e.g. SAPOL, 2023, p. 6).

Police jurisdictions also have different management approaches to property intended to be used as court exhibits. For instance, in Queensland, officers are encouraged to minimise inconvenience to owners whose property may have been seized as evidence and consider returning exhibits unless there are compelling reasons not to or where the outcome of the case would be affected (Queensland Police Service, 2024, p. 7). Exhibits of evidentiary value that are related to homicides must be retained for up to 100 years (Queensland Police Service, 2024, p. 7). In Victoria, officers must take reasonable steps to return property if reasons for seizure no longer exist (*Victoria Police Act 2013* (Vic) s 272). Similarly, section 218 of the *Law Enforcement (Powers and Responsibilities) Act 2002* (NSW) mandates that NSW police return property to a lawful owner if the officer is satisfied; it is not required to be obtained as evidence. The police also have storage retention policies. The South Australian Police General Order Property, for example, provides that property in SAPOL custody for investigatory or evidentiary purposes must not be released or disposed of except for scientific analysis or where the property is no longer required for use in connection with legal proceedings or official investigations, and it has been one month since legal proceedings concluded (SAPOL, 2023, p. 5). In Victoria, police briefs of evidence can be destroyed seven years after a criminal case has concluded, and records of evidence, which were not included in the brief, such as audiovisual recordings, can be destroyed after administrative use (Public Record Office Victoria, 2024, pp. 21, 25).

The risks arising from Australia's patchwork evidence storage systems were highlighted in 2013, when exhibits related to 22 unsolved homicide cases in New South Wales were unexpectedly found in a storeroom at the Sydney Police Centre (McKinnell, 2023). The commissioner of a subsequent 2023 inquiry into LGBTQ+ hate crimes described police record-keeping practices as 'bordering on shambolic' (Sackar, 2023a, b, p. 4349). The report highlighted significant issues, including the misfiling, contamination, destruction, or return of physical exhibits (Special Commission, 2023, p. 1345). Most jurisdictions have instigated improvements in security and standards for the storage of forensic exhibits (see e.g., Auditor General Western Australia, 2013). However, the lack of visibility of storage practices, particularly the number of locations across which evidence can be stored, creates an ongoing risk that evidence that may be crucial for post-conviction review has been lost or destroyed. The destruction of exculpatory material has contributed to numerous miscarriages of justice in the United Kingdom (Westminster Commission on Miscarriages of Justice, 2021). In Australia, widespread inadequate and inappropriate property storage practices by police and storage retention limits likely contribute to unresolved wrongful convictions.

Legislation

Criminal Procedure Act 2009 (Vic)
Law Enforcement (Powers and Responsibilities) Act 2002 (NSW)
Victoria Police Act 2013 (Vic)

Cases

Anile v The Queen [2018] VSCA 235
Cannon v Tahche (2002) VR 317
DPP v Galloway (A Pseudonym) and Others [2014] VSCA 272
Eastman v Director of Public Prosecutions (No.13) [2016] ACTCA 65
El Bayeh v The Queen (2011) 206 A Crim R 541
Grey v the Queen (2001) 75 ALJR 1708
Mallard v The Queen (2005) 224 CLR 125
Orman v The Queen (2019) 59 VR 511
R v Button [2001] QCA 133
R v Ernst [2020] QCA 150
R v Farquharson (2009) 26 VR 410
R v Jama [2009] VSCA, unrep, 7 December 2009
R v Keogh (No 2) [2014] SASCFC 136
R v *Smith [No 1]* [2011] NSWSC 725
Roberts v The Queen [2020] VSCA 58

References

Akinci, C., & Sadler-Smith, E. (2020). 'If something doesn't look right, go find out why': How intuitive decision making is accomplished in police first-response. *European Journal of Work and Organizational Psychology, 29*(1), 78–92.

Alketbi, S. K. (2024). DNA contamination in crime scene investigations: Common errors, best practices, and insights from a survey study. *Biomedical Journal of Scientific & Technical Research, 58*(5), 50970–50982.

Boulton, L., & Cole, J. (2016). Adaptive flexibility: Examining the role of expertise in the decision making of authorized firearms officers during armed confrontation. *Journal of Cognitive Engineering and Decision Making, 10*(3), 291–308.

Commonwealth Director of Public Prosecutions "CDPP". (2017). *Statement on disclosure.* Retrieved 07/11/2024 from https://www.cdpp.gov.au/sites/default/files/Disclosure%20Statement-March-2017_0.pdf

Cordner, G., & Scott, M. S. (2014). Police discretion and its control. *Encyclopedia of criminology and criminal justice*, 3587–3596.

Corruption and Crime Commission and the Western Australia Police. (2005). *Report of a Joint Inquiry by Western Australia Police and the Corruption and Crime Commission.* https://www.ccc.wa.gov.au/sites/default/files/Western%20Australia%20Police%20Property%20Management%20Practices.pdf

Delémont, O., Bitzer, S., Jendly, M., & Ribaux, O. (2017). The practice of crime scene examination in an intelligence-based perspective. In *The Routledge international handbook of forensic intelligence and criminology* (pp. 86–101). Routledge.

Dioso-Villa, R. (2015). A repository of wrongful convictions in Australia: First steps toward estimating prevalence and causal contributing factors. *Flinders Law Journal, 17*(2), 163–202.

Eastman Inquiry. (2014). *Inquiry into the Conviction of David Harold Eastman for the Murder of Colin Stanley Winchester: Report of the Board of Inquiry.* https://www.courts.act.gov.au/__data/assets/pdf_file/0010/977680/eastman_inquiry_-_board_of_inquiry_redacted_full_report_29_may_2014.pdf

General, W. A. A. (2013). *Western Australian Auditor General's Report, Follow-up Performance Audit of Behind the Evidence: Forensic Services.* https://audit.wa.gov.au/wp-content/uploads/report2013_08.pdf

Gould, J. B., Senn, S. L., Lowrey-Kimberg, B., & Phiri, L. (2021). Mapping the path of Brady violations: Typologies, causes & consequences in erroneous conviction cases. *Syracuse Law Review, 71*, 1061.

Julian, R., Kelty, S., & Robertson, J. (2012). "Get it right the first time": Critical issues at the crime scene. *Current Issues in Criminal Justice, 24*(1), 25–37.

Justice Committee. (2018). *Disclosure of evidence in criminal cases inquiry.* House of Commons. Retrieved 07/11/2024 from https://committees.parliament.uk/work/3630/disclosure-of-evidence-in-criminal-cases-inquiry/publications/

Kelty, S. F., Julian, R., & Robertson, J. (2011). Professionalism in crime scene examination: The seven key attributes of top crime scene examiners. *Forensic Science Policy & Management: An International Journal, 2*(4), 175–186.

Leach, I. (2023). 'It's on my head': Risk and accountability in public order policing. *The Police Journal, 96*(1), 61–82.

McCartney, C., & Shorter, L. (2019). Exacerbating injustice: Post-conviction disclosure in England and Wales. *International Journal of Law, Crime and Justice, 59*, 100323.

McCartney, C., & Shorter, L. (2020). Police retention and storage of evidence in England and Wales. *International Journal of Police Science & Management, 22*(2), 123–136.

McCartney, C., & Shorter, L. (2023). 'You don't know what you've got 'til it's gone': Police retention of investigative materials. *International Journal of Police Science & Management*, 14613557231203493.

McKinnell, J. (2023, 6/09/2023). How police stumbled upon "vital" evidence used to convicted Family Court bomber Leonard John Warwick. *ABC News*. https://www.abc.net.au/news/2023-09-06/evidence-used-to-convict-family-court-bomber-found-by-chance/102818660

McMurdo, M. A. (2020). Royal Commission into the Management of Police Informants. *Final Report*. V. Government. rcmpi.vic.gov.au/final-report

National Registry of Exonerations. (2020). *Government Misconduct and Convicting the Innocent: The Role of Prosecutors, Police and Other Law Enforcement*. National Registry of Exonerations. Retrieved 07/11/2024 from https://www.law.umich.edu/special/exoneration/Documents/Government_Misconduct_and_Convicting_the_Innocent.pdf

Plater, D., & De Vreeze, L. (2012). Is the golden rule of full prosecution disclosure a modern mission impossible. *Flinders LJ, 14*, 133.

Police Integrity Commission. (2017). *Project harlequin*. https://www.opengov.nsw.gov.au/publications/16714

Polykarpou, M. (2022). Prosecutorial and police disclosure ethics in criminal evidence review in the UK and the US. A comparative account. *Criminal Justice Ethics, 41*(1), 45–61.

Public Record Office Victoria. (2024). Victoria Police retention and disposal authority: Pros 10/14. In Operational Procedures Manual (OPM) Issue 100.1 Public Edition, Effective 24 June 2024, Chapter 4, § Chapter 4 (2024). https://www.police.qld.gov.au/sites/default/files/2024-06/OPM-ch.4-Property_0.pdf

Ruyters, M., Stratton, G., & Bartle, J. (2021). The culture of non-disclosure and miscarriages of justice. *Alternative Law Journal, 1037969X20987009*, 299.

Sackar, J. (2023a). Special Commission of Inquiry into LGBTIQ hate crimes Volume 3. S. C. o. I. i. L. h. crimes. https://www.nsw.gov.au/sites/default/files/2023-12/SCOI-LGBTIQ-Hate-Crimes-Volume-3-191223.pdf

Sackar, J. (2023b). *Transcript of Proceedings, Special Commission of Inquiry into LGBTIQ hate crimes, 20 June 2023*. Retrieved 07/11/2024 from https://lgbtiq.specialcommission.nsw.gov.au/assets/lgbtiq/transcripts/TRA.00062.00001.pdf

Shorter, L., & Madland, G. (2019). 'Let them have it!' A review of the retention and storage of, and access to, material post conviction in England and Wales. *Medicine, Science and the Law, 59*(4), 223–231.

Smith, M., & Urbas, G. (2019). A century of science in Australian criminal trials. *Australian Bar Review, 47*, 72–85.

South Australia Police (SAPOL). (2023). *General Order Property*. Retrieved from https://www.police.sa.gov.au/__data/assets/pdf_file/0020/1306163/Doc-1-General-Order-Property-24-1775_Redacted.PDF

Strom, K. J., Hickman, M. J., & Ropero-Miller, J. D. (2011). Evidence retention policies in US law enforcement agencies: Implications for unsolved cases and postconviction DNA testing. *Journal of Contemporary Criminal Justice, 27*(2), 133–148.

van den Eeden, C. A., de Poot, C. J., & Van Koppen, P. J. (2016). Forensic expectations: Investigating a crime scene with prior information. *Science & Justice, 56*(6), 475–481.

Van den Eeden, C. A., Ost, J., de Poot, C. J., & van Koppen, P. J. (2018). Solving the puzzle: The effects of contextual information and feedback on the interpretation of a crime scene. *Journal of Investigative Psychology and Offender Profiling, 15*(2), 109–123.

Victoria Police. (2024). *Specialist roles and areas for police officers.* Retrieved 07/11/2024 from https://www.police.vic.gov.au/specialist-areas

Victorian Auditor-General's Office (VAGO). (2018). *Police management of property and exhibits.* In. Melbourne: Victorian Auditor-General's Office (VAGO).

Vincent, F. H. R. (2010). *Report: Inquiry into the circumstances that led to the conviction of Mr Farah Abdulkadir Jama* (March 2010). V. G. Printer.

Westminster Commission on Miscarriages of Justice. (2021). *In the interest of justice: An inquiry into the criminal cases review commission.* https://appgmiscarriagesofjustice.wordpress.com/commission-on-miscarriages-of-justice/

CHAPTER 6

Use of Unreliable Evidence: Forensic and Identification Error

Abstract This chapter critically examines the cultural and institutional practices that sustain the use of forensic science and identification evidence despite longstanding awareness of their potential to contribute to wrongful convictions. We explore how courtroom norms, judicial gatekeeping, and perceptions about the expertise of witnesses enable the admission of unreliable evidence. The chapter highlights the cultural defence to expertise, the limitations of legal safeguards, and the challenges faced by jurors and defence lawyers in assessing forensic validity. Through case studies such as Gordon Wood and Kathleen Folbigg, the chapter reveals how legal culture, institutional inertia, and epistemic gaps between science and law combine to perpetuate risky evidentiary practice. The chapter also addresses the well-recognised fallibility of identification evidence, a leading cause of wrongful conviction internationally, through case studies like Terry Irving and Vincent Narkle. we underscore the potential for miscarriages of justice arising from flawed identification practices. These practices reflect systemic overconfidence in eyewitness reliability. High-profile Australian cases underscore how the criminal justice system often fails to safeguard against these risks, revealing a culture of deference to certain forms of evidence despite their known fallibility. Ultimately, this chapter emphasises the critical need for robust gatekeeping mechanisms and a cautious approach to these seemingly compelling, yet often unreliable, forms of evidence in the pursuit of justice.

M. Ruyters et al., *Innocence Unveiled*,
https://doi.org/10.1007/978-3-031-91343-3_6

Keywords Wrong convictions • Unreliable evidence • Forensic science error • Identification evidence • Junk science • Reliability

Unreliable evidence is a significant factor in wrongful convictions. There are numerous recognised categories of potentially unreliable evidence in Australia. This chapter considers the risks associated with the use of unreliable forensic science and identification evidence. Both are highly persuasive for juries, emphasising the critical need for effective gatekeeping. Techniques such as hair comparison and bite mark analysis, for instance, have been discredited, raising concerns about the ongoing use of unreliable or 'junk science' in courtrooms. Gordon Wood's conviction based on unqualified biomechanical expert opinion evidence is a key example of the dangers of admitting evidence that lacks scientific rigour. Australian courts have also long recognised the dangers of identification evidence, which has a significant persuasive impact on juries but is prone to errors influenced by factors such as poor lighting, brief observations, and suggestive procedures.

While police informer evidence is typically discussed in the context of unreliable evidence, the use of informers is addressed in Chap. 11, where we consider the difficulties in balancing the need for police to use investigative techniques against defendants' right to access information relevant to their defence.

Forensic Evidence

Morgan's study of wrongful conviction cases in the United States National Registry of Exonerations found that 635 of 732 cases involved a case error associated with forensic science, and 491 cases in which a forensic science error contributed to the wrongful conviction (2023, p. 919). These errors included omissions in forensic science reports, classification errors, and misrepresentation of forensic evidence by prosecutors. Experts, particularly in the forensic sciences, can have a substantial impact on criminal trial outcomes. Misuse or misrepresentation of their testimony and opinions based on unreliable science, however, can lead to wrongful convictions. There are specific rules for the admissibility of expert testimony in Australia. Under section 79 of the *Uniform Evidence Acts* ("UAE"), for instance, expert opinion is admissible if it is based on specialised knowledge derived from training, study, or experience. Despite these legal safeguards, there are growing concerns about the admissibility, reliability, and interpretation of forensic evidence, which have prompted increased scrutiny of the use and regulation of expert testimony.

Numerous forensic techniques, such as hair comparison analysis and bite mark analysis, have also come under scrutiny due to their lack of scientific reliability (Bush et al., 2023; Smith & Goodman, 1995; Weinberg, 2021). Researchers have noted that judges often admit expert testimony with limited scrutiny of its reliability, relying on the perceived expertise of witnesses rather than a rigorous assessment of the reliability of forensic science evidence (e.g. Edmond & Roque, 2012; Hamer & Edmond, 2019; Martire & Edmond, 2017). The willingness to admit expert evidence places the onus on juries to assess the weight of the evidence during a trial, often without sufficient guidance on how to evaluate its scientific validity (Edmond et al., 2023; Glazebrook, 2018; Hamer & Edmond, 2019). Cross examination, which is intended to expose weaknesses in expert testimony, is also often ineffective in forensic cases. Defence lawyers frequently lack the resources or expertise to thoroughly challenge the scientific validity of the evidence (Edmond et al., 2018, p. 867). There have also been concerns about the impact of the alleged phenomenon of the "CSI effect," where jurors have inflated expectations about forensic science due to media portrayals. Jurors may overvalue forensic evidence without fully understanding its limitations, leading to misguided verdicts (Biju et al., 2021; Martire et al., 2019; Schweitzer & Saks, 2007). However, recent research suggests that jurors may be less influenced by popular portrayals of forensic science than previously believed (Eatley et al., 2016; Klentz et al., 2020).

A notable example of inept expert evidence occurred in Gordon Wood's case. Wood was convicted of murdering his girlfriend, Caroline Byrne, in 1995. Byrne died after falling from The Gap, a notorious cliff in Sydney (*Wood v The Queen* "Wood" [2012] NSWCCA 21 [1]). Wood's conviction was largely based on forensic evidence provided by Associate Professor Rod Cross, a plasma physicist. Cross conducted a series of biomechanical experiments aiming to prove that Byrne was thrown to her death 'rather than having voluntarily jumped' (*Wood,* 2012, [469]) and testified that Wood must have "spear-thrown" Byrne off the cliff ([320]). Cross subsequently wrote a book about Wood's case. On appeal, McClellan CJ observed that Cross had no qualifications or experience in biomechanics but 'was allowed, without objection, to express opinions outside his field of specialized knowledge' ([467]–[468]). Further, Cross had assumed the role of investigator and become 'an active participant in attempting to prove' that Wood had committed murder [758].

Wood's conviction highlighted existing concerns about adequate gatekeeping in admitting forensic science evidence, particularly about its reliability.

Junk Science

The term 'junk science' refers to a claim presented as scientifically validated, but which is false or misleading (Turvey, 2013, p. 171). Concerns regarding the admissibility of junk science in criminal cases have been present since the 1980s. However, junk science received significant attention after the 2009 report by the US National Academy of Forensic Sciences, which found that many forensic techniques used to provide expert opinion within US courts had not established the validity of their approaches or their accuracy (National Research Council, 2009, p. 86). Following this ground-breaking report, there has been a surge in research attempting to improve the scientific credibility of forensic science disciplines globally (Kolowski et al., 2016).

In some forensic science subfields, scientific reviews revealed that available empirical evidence did not support expert claims, leading to discredited protocols or principles being abandoned. For some disciplines, greater scientific evaluation led to a move away from exaggerated claims or the greater use of caveats when providing expert testimony. For example, microscopic hair comparisons, previously used to definitively match crime scenes and suspect samples, are now more commonly used to narrow down a set of hairs for DNA analysis or to note morphological characteristics of hair, such as distinguishing animal and human hair (National Research Council, 2009, p. 161). In contrast, disciplines such as forensic DNA identification have withstood scientific scrutiny effectively and have been further reinforced by research (Edwards, 2014, pp. 5, 6).

Nevertheless, some forensic disciplines and techniques continue to be presented in criminal trials despite a continued lack of scientific evidence or research indicating they are 'junk science.' For example, despite being discredited following scientific scrutiny, forensic bite mark identification continued to be admitted into evidence in common law courts (Saks & Koehler, 2005). The unreliability of bite mark analysis was highlighted in the high-profile 1985 conviction of Australian man Raymond John Carrol. Carroll's conviction for the murder of 17-month-old Deidre Kennedy, whose body was found with bite marks, was based on forensic odontologists' testimony that Carroll's dentistry was a 'definite match' to the bite marks. The Court of Appeal held that evidence of Carroll's propensity to bite children's legs was prejudicial, and Carroll was acquitted (Parkinson, 2003). New evidence indicated that Carroll had killed Deirdre, but at the time Carroll could not be re-tried for murder due to the law relating the double jeopardy, and Carroll was instead charged and convicted of perjury (Parkinson, 2003, pp. 603–604).

In Australia, almost all government forensic science laboratories are NATA[1] accredited and use proficiency testing to ensure that forensic disciplines and techniques meet appropriate standards of reliability and validity, and that expert evidence is presented with sufficient understanding of the limitations and error rates associated with specific techniques (Wilson-Wilde et al., 2017, pp. 55–56). A 2017 analysis of error rates for proficiency tests in Australia, however, consistently found persistent errors, even when practitioners were aware they were participating in proficiency testing (Wilson-Wilde et al., 2017). Wilson-Wilde, Smith, and Bruenisholz (2017) analysed 2914 proficiency tests undertaken between 2005 and 2015 by Australian government forensic science service providers, and found numerous errors, including transcription and attribution errors, and errors resulting in false positive or false negatives (see also Wilson-Wilde et al., 2019).

Concerns were raised in the cases of Robert Farquharson and Kathleen Folbigg about convictions based on unreliable scientific evidence (Bachelard et al., 2024). Farquharson was convicted of murdering his three children by driving them into a dam. Expert opinion evidence of cough syncope was called by the prosecution to exclude Farquharson's claim that he had blacked out after a coughing fit (*R v Farquharson* [2009] VSCA 307 [16]). Crown also led engineering and reconstruction evidence to show that Farquharson would have been in control of his vehicle [25]. This evidence was included as a "drive through" experiment [27]. Farquharson was convicted by juries in 2007 and 2010 (*DPP v Farquharson* [2007] VSC 469; *R v Farquharson* [2010] VSC 462).

Kathleen Folbigg was convicted in 2003 of the homicides of her four infant children. Central to her conviction was a discredited theory known as "Meadow's Law" that 'one infant death is a tragedy, two is suspicious, and three is murder' (*R v Sally Clark* [2003] EWCA 2010). The

[1] National Association of Testing Authorities.

paediatrician who coined the dictum, Professor Roy Meadow, was later struck off the medical register in 2005, however, following misconduct charges arising from his role as a prosecution witness in three trials of women who were wrongfully accused of killing their children (Dyer, 2004, 2005). A 2022 inquiry subsequently found there was medical evidence that her children died of natural causes (Bathurst, 2022, p. 415).

The admission of potentially unreliable expert opinion evidence is managed through judicial gatekeeping, cross examination, and the use of rebuttal experts to challenge the suspect expert evidence (Edmond & Roque, 2012). While it has been clear since *IMM v The Queen* (2016) 257 CLR 300 [54] that questions of the reliability of evidence are for the jury, judges can consider the reliability of an expert opinion when determining whether there is a danger of unfair prejudice to the accused (*R v Bowie (No 1)* [2022] NSWSC 1502, [67], Yehia J; *Evidence Act 2008* (Vic) s 137). The trustworthiness of the evidence will be based on its scientific validity (*Tuite v The Queen* [2015] VSCA 148 [101]). While the "epistemic competence" of judges to interpret and assess the validity of expert opinions has been questioned (Dillon, 2017; Martire, 2023), Martire and Montgomery-Farrer have found some evidence that judges can distinguish between high- and low-quality expert opinions (Martire & Montgomery-Farrer, 2020).

Reliability of Evidence: Witness Misidentification

The Australian Law Reform Commission noted in 1986 that identification evidence 'had been recognised for some time as amongst the most unreliable and potentially dangerous categories of evidence' (ALRC, 1985, p xxxvii).' According to the US National Registry of Exonerations (2024a, b), 27% of exonerations resulted from mistaken witness identification. This figure corresponds to data from the Canadian Registry of Wrongful Convictions (2024), which recorded 25 mistaken eyewitness cases from 89 wrongful convictions (approximately 28%). Australian courts have adopted a cautious approach to identification evidence given the potential prejudice or unfairness to the accused with Murphy J observing in *Alexander v The Queen* (1981) 145 CLR 395 (p. 435), that '[m]iscarriages of justice arising from mistaken identifications (even by numerous witnesses) are part of our folklore.'

Types of Identification Evidence

Visual identification evidence can be made through identification parades, dock identifications; in-court comparisons between the accused person and CCTV images; picture identification evidence; and photo board identification. In criminal matters, identification evidence is generally divided into several distinct categories. Positive identification involves a witness identifying the accused person as someone they had seen previously (*Festa v The Queen* (2001) CLR 593). The most common example of this would be a witness identifying an accused from a police photo board or digital identification parade (Rubínová et al., 2021; *Festa v The Queen* (2001) 208 CLR 592; *R v Carpenter* [2011] ACTSC 71, [95]). Recognition evidence, on the other hand, is based on a person's previous familiarity with the accused's evidence. This is evidence that they recognised the person committing the offence based on knowing the accused (*Davies and Cody v The King* (1937) 57 CLR 170; *Trudgett v The Queen* [2008] NSWCCA 62). Recognition evidence and positive identification evidence also fall under section 35 *Jury Directions Act 2015* (Vic). In contrast, negative identification can be evidence that the defendant is not the person who committed the offence (e.g. *Kanaan and Others v The Queen* [2006] NSWCCA 109). Negative identification evidence may even identify someone else as the person who committed the offence. Witnesses can also give aural identification evidence (*Bulejcik v The Queen* (1996) 185 CLR; *R v Callaghan* (2001) 4 VR 79).

Witnesses can also provide evidence of similarities between the accused and the offender, such as a unique scent, accent, or gait (*Festa v The Queen* (2001) 208 CLR 592; *Jury Directions Act 2015* (Vic) s 35), or comparison evidence, which involves a non-expert comparing two people or characteristics such as the defendant's voice in court with a recording of the defendant's voice. Experts, including ad hoc experts, give opinion evidence rather than identification evidence (*Nasrallah v The Queen, R v Nasrallah* [2015] NSWCCA 188; *R v Leung and Wong* [1999] NSWCCA 287). Ad hoc expertise can be acquired, for instance, by listening to a recording several times to become more familiar (*Butera v Director of Public Prosecutions* (1987) 164 CLR 180, 195; *Irani v The Queen* [2008] NSWCCA 217). This issue arose in the case of *Davey v Tasmania* "Davey" (2020) 35 Tas R 362. Matthew Davey was jointly tried for stealing offences and aggravated burglary. The prosecution-led evidence of intercepted telephone calls, including opinion evidence given by Detective Jago identifying voices heard on telephone intercept recordings. Jago's evidence was that he was not familiar with Davey's voice prior to the investigation but he had listened to between 720 and 1200 intercepted calls and had identified Davey by comparing the voice in those calls with Davey's voice in Davey's police interview with Jago (p. 378). Davey had also identified himself in several calls and there were other markers of identity such as calls in which the names "Matthew, Matty or Matthew Davey were used" (p. 380). Davey unsuccessfully argued on appeal that the trial judge should not have admitted Jago's evidence (see also *Tran v The Queen; Chang v The Queen* [2016] VSCA 79). In these cases, we would argue that, given the police investment in a conviction outcome, it would be preferable to obtain expert comparison evidence.

Dangers of Identification Evidence

Witness identification evidence can be highly persuasive to a jury but may be unreliable when influenced by factors such as brief observations, poor lighting, the time gap between witnessing the offender and making the subsequent identification, and memory challenges. Witnesses can also be susceptible to suggestion, so it is desirable that witnesses identify the accused as early as possible after the event (*Alexander v The Queen* "Alexander" (1981) 145 CLR 395, p. 399, Gibbs CJ). For instance, a witness identifying someone from police records might be swayed by the knowledge that the person has a criminal record, and a similar bias could occur if the identification is made while the person is in police custody. In *Alexander* (1981, p. 409), Stephen J also warned about a "displacement effect", in that a witness's memory of a photo they have been shown might displace their original memory, with the result that they match any subsequent face-to-face identification to the photo rather than their original memory.

Australian courts give juries warnings about the dangers of admitting identification evidence, and identification parades are regarded as the 'safest and most satisfactory' means of ensuring an accurate visual identification (*Alexander,* 1981, p. 400, Gibbs CJ). This is affirmed in s114 *UEA*, which provides that visual identification evidence (this does not include picture identification evidence), will not be admissible unless an identification parade was held before the identification was made.

Curiously, despite the recognition of the dangers of identification evidence and the potential for misidentification, there are relatively few recorded Australian cases of wrongful convictions in which misidentification was a determining factor. Terry Irving's case is often referred to in this context; however, the primary issue on appeal was the failure of the prosecution to lead—and the failure of the defence to cross examine on—witnesses' out-of-court identifications. Terry Irving, an Indigenous man from North Queensland, was convicted of armed robbery in 1993. The main issue in the case against him was the identity of the person who robbed the bank (*Irving v The Queen* "Irving" [1997] HCATrans 251). Six eyewitnesses were presented with photo boards, each containing 12 photographs for identification. The identification process was videotaped and transcribed, but the jury at the trial was not provided with the results of these identifications (p. 405). Irving was unrepresented in his unsuccessful appeal. On subsequent appeal to the High Court in 1997, Irving's defence argued that the prosecution should have led the identification evidence, which showed that four of the six witnesses who had claimed to identify Irving in court had not identified Irving in the out-of-court identification. Further, none of the five witnesses who identified the shirt worn by the armed robber in court had identified the shirt in the out-of-court identification (p. 405). The police officer who conducted the identification procedures did not give evidence at the trial and, consequently, was not available to be cross-examined about the procedures. Other material considered by the High Court included a witness's statement that police had shown her a still from a bank video camera despite police advising Irving's solicitor that the bank video camera had malfunctioned. His conviction was overturned by the High Court, and the prosecution discontinued the prosecution a few days later.

In the case of Vincent Narkle, the potential unreliability of a witness's identification was in question as the police had failed to disclose an earlier identification, but it was not established whether this might have been a misidentification or a mistaken identification. Vincent Narkle, an Indigenous man from Western Australia, was convicted of sexual assault in 1993. The complainant had been assaulted by two men on 28 April 1992. She had not met either accused previously and gave evidence of identifying Narkle and his co-accused from photo boards on 26 May 1992. Following a complaint however, the Western Australia Police Internal Affairs Unit found that the complainant had identified Narkle as a suspect from photos and by name through entries in a police journal almost one month prior to the photo board identification (*Narkle v The State of*

Western Australia [2006] WASCA 113, [4], [5], [9]). The police had shown her the photos a few times before the photo board identification.

The police had failed to disclose the journal to the prosecutor or defence, depriving the defence of an opportunity to cross-examine the police and complainant. On appeal, Narkle argued that, had the defence been able to cross-examine on the prior identification, the utility of the photo board identification would have been diminished. The photo board identification evidence would then have attracted a jury warning or potentially been excluded ([10]). The Western Australia Court of Appeal found that the non-disclosure had led to a miscarriage of justice, set aside the conviction, and ordered a judgment of acquittal in respect of each charge.

In Frank Button's case, however, while his appeal on a rape conviction turned on DNA retesting that identified another person as the perpetrator, the complainant's mistaken identification of him was the primary evidence against him at trial. Analysis prior to the trial had failed to establish a DNA profile from samples taken from the complainant, and investigating authorities had failed to test bedding from the bed where the offence occurred (*R v Button* [2001] QCA 133).

Andrew Mallard's case also involved identification evidence (*Mallard v The Queen* (2005) 224 CLR 125). Katherine Barsden's description of the person she saw outside the victim's jewellery shop did not match Mallard, and she failed to identify Mallard from a photo board (Corruption and Crime Commission, 2008, p. 89). Lily Raine identified Mallard from a photo board as the person she saw in a lift near the jewellery shop, but the reliability of that identification was affected by her having seen Mallard arrested (Corruption and Crime Commission, 2008, pp. 95–96).

Witness misidentifications usually happen early in police investigations (Wixted et al., 2021). Accurate identifications can be affected by stress experienced by the witness at the time of identification (Deffenbacher et al., 2004), susceptibility of memory to misinformation (Loftus, 2005), diminution of memory over time (O'Neill Shermer et al., 2011), the witness's confidence in making the first identification (Quigley-McBride & Wells, 2023), and the length of time the witness viewed the accused at the relevant time (Memon et al., 2003). Cross-racial identifications are also less reliable than own-race identifications (Katzman & Kovera, 2023; Meissner & Brigham, 2001; Stenzel, 2016). Kleider-Offutt et al. found that possessing stereotypical features may be a contributing factor to witness misidentification for black men (Kleider-Offutt et al., 2017).

Legislation

Uniform Evidence Acts
Evidence Act 2008 (Vic)
Jury Directions Act 2015 (Vic)

Cases

Alexander v The Queen (1981) 145 CLR 395
Bulejcik v The Queen (1996) 185 CLR
Butera v Director of Public Prosecutions (1987) 164 CLR 180
Davies and Cody v The King (1937) 57 CLR 170
Davey v Tasmania (2020) 35 Tas R 362*Festa v The Queen* (2001) 208 CLR 592
IMM v The Queen (2016) 257 CLR 300
Irani v The Queen [2008] NSWCCA 217
Irving v The Queen [1997] HCATrans 251, 15 August 1997
Kanaan and Others v The Queen [2006] NSWCCA 109
Mallard v The Queen (2005) 224 CLR 125
Narkle v The State of Western Australia [2006] WASCA 113
Nasrallah v The Queen, R v Nasrallah [2015] NSWCCA 188
R v Carpenter [2011a] ACTSC 71
R v Bowie (No 1) [2022] NSWSC 1502
R v Button [2001] QCA 133
R v Callaghan (2001) 4 VR 79
R v Carpenter [2011b] ACTSC 71
R v Farquharson [2007] VSC 469
R v Farquharson (2009) 26 VR 410
R v Farquharson [2010] VSC 462
R v Leung and Wong [1999] NSWCCA 287
R v Sally Clark [2003] EWCA 2010
Tran v The Queen; Chang v The Queen [2016] VSCA 79
Trudgett v The Queen [2008] NSWCCA 62
Tuite v The Queen [2015] VSCA 148
Wood v The Queen [2012] NSWCCA 21

References

Australian Law Reform Commission. (1985). Report No. 26 Interim: Evidence Volume 1.

Bachelard, M., McKenzie, N., & Schwartz, R. (2024). *'It could be any one of us': Top scientists sound alarm over unreliable evidence.* https://www.theage.com.au/national/victoria/it-could-be-any-of-us-top-scientists-sound-alarm-over-unreliable-evidence-20240528-p5jh7q.html

Bathurst, T. (2022). *2022 inquiry into the convictions of Kathleen Megan Folbigg*. N. Government. https://2022folbigginquiry.dcj.nsw.gov.au/content/dam/dcj/2022-folbigg-inquiry/documents/Report_of_the_2022_Inquiry_into_the_convictions_of_Kathleen_Megan_Folbigg.pdf

Biju, A., Hambly, K., & Joshi, A. (2021). The complexity of forensic science in criminal investigations: Is there a gold standard? *Voices of Forensic Science, 1*(1), 7–26.

Bush, M. A., Miller, R. G., & Bush, P. J. (2023). CE credit. Bitemark analysis: The legal vs scientific battle for justice. *Journal of the California Dental Association, 51*(1), 2191391.

Canadian Registry of Wrongful Convictions. (2024). *Wrongful convictions data visualized*. https://www.wrongfulconvictions.ca/data

Corruption and Crime Commission. (2008). *Report on the Inquiry Into Alleged Misconduct by Public Officers in Connection with the Investigation of the Murder of Mrs Pamela Lawrence, the Prosecution and Appeals of Mr Andrew Mark Mallard, and Other Related Matters*. C. a. C. Commission. ccc.wa.gov.au/node/637

Deffenbacher, K. A., Bornstein, B. H., Penrod, S. D., & McGorty, E. K. (2004). A meta-analytic review of the effects of high stress on eyewitness memory. *Law and Human Behavior, 28*, 687–706.

Dillon, J. R. (2017). Expertise on trial. *The Columbia Science and Technology Law Review, 19*, 247.

Dyer, O. (2004). *Meadow faces GMC over evidence given in child death cases*. British Medical Journal Publishing Group.

Dyer, C. (2005). *Professor Roy meadow struck off*. British Medical Journal Publishing Group.

Eatley, G., Hueston, H. H., & Price, K. (2016). A meta-analysis of the CSI effect: The impact of popular media on jurors' perception of forensic evidence. *Politics, Bureaucracy & Justice, 5*(2).

Edmond, G., & Roque, M. S. (2012). The cool crucible: Forensic science and the frailty of the criminal trial. *Current Issues in Criminal Justice, 24*(1), 51–68.

Edmond, G., Cunliffe, E., Martire, K., & San Roque, M. (2018). Forensic science evidence and the limits of cross-examination. *The Melbourne University Law Review, 42*, 858.

Edmond, G., Chin, J. M., Martire, K. A., & Roque, M. S. (2023). A warning about judicial directions and warnings. *TheAdelaide Law Review, 44*(1), 194–245.

Edwards, H. T. (2014). *Reflections on the findings of the National Academy of Sciences Committee on Identifying the Needs of the Forensic Science Community, First Public Meeting of the National Commission on Forensic Science, February 3, 2014*. In: National Commission on Forensic Science.

Glazebrook, S. (2018). Miscarriage by expert. *Victoria University of Wellington Law Review, 49*, 245.

Hamer, D., & Edmond, G. (2019). Forensic science evidence, wrongful convictions and adversarial process. *University of Queensland Law Journal, 38*, 185.

Katzman, J., & Kovera, M. B. (2023). Potential causes of racial disparities in wrongful convictions based on mistaken identifications: Own-race bias and differences in evidence-based suspicion. *Law and Human Behavior, 47*(1), 23.

Kleider-Offutt, H. M., Knuycky, L. R., Clevinger, A. M., & Capodanno, M. M. (2017). Wrongful convictions and prototypical black features: Can a face-type facilitate misidentifications? *Legal and Criminological Psychology, 22*(2), 350–358.

Klentz, B. A., Winters, G. M., & Chapman, J. E. (2020). The CSI effect and the impact of DNA evidence on mock jurors and jury deliberations. *Psychology, Crime & Law, 26*(6), 552–570.

Kolowski, J., Barden, C., Brown, C., Leete, J., & Czyryca, C. (2016). Proficiency testing trends following the 2009 National Academy of Sciences Report, "Strengthening Forensic Science in the United States: A Path Forward". *Forensic Science Policy & Management: An International Journal, 7*(3–4), 98–105.

Loftus, E. F. (2005). Planting misinformation in the human mind: A 30-year investigation of the malleability of memory. *Learning & Memory, 12*(4), 361–366.

Martire, K. (2023). In what way are you qualified? Understanding epistemic (in) competence and expert persuasion through the courtroom of my cousin Vinny. *Journal of Expertise/June, 6*(3).

Martire, K. A., & Edmond, G. (2017). Rethinking expert opinion evidence. *Melbourne University Law Review, 40*(3), 967–998.

Martire, K. A., & Montgomery-Farrer, B. (2020). Judging experts: Australian magistrates' evaluations of expert opinion quality. *Psychiatry, Psychology and Law, 27*(6), 950–962.

Martire, K. A., Ballantyne, K. N., Bali, A., Edmond, G., Kemp, R. I., & Found, B. (2019). Forensic science evidence: Naive estimates of false positive error rates and reliability. *Forensic Science International, 302*, 109877.

Meissner, C. A., & Brigham, J. C. (2001). Thirty years of investigating the own-race bias in memory for faces: A meta-analytic review. *Psychology, Public Policy, and Law, 7*(1), 3.

Memon, A., Hope, L., & Bull, R. (2003). Exposure duration: Effects on eyewitness accuracy and confidence. *British Journal of Psychology, 94*(3), 339–354.

Morgan, J. (2023). Wrongful convictions and claims of false or misleading forensic evidence. *Journal of Forensic Sciences, 68*(3), 908–961.

National Research Council. (2009). *Strengthening forensic science in the United States: A path forward*. National Academies Press.

O'Neill Shermer, L., Rose, K. C., & Hoffman, A. (2011). Perceptions and credibility: Understanding the nuances of eyewitness testimony. *Journal of Contemporary Criminal Justice, 27*(2), 183–203.

Parkinson, C. (2003). Double jeopardy reform: The new evidence exception for acquittals. *UNSWLJ, 26*, 603.

Quigley-McBride, A., & Wells, G. L. (2023). Eyewitness confidence and decision time reflect identification accuracy in actual police lineups. *Law and Human Behavior, 47*(2), 333.

Rubínová, E., Fitzgerald, R. J., Juncu, S., Ribbers, E., Hope, L., & Sauer, J. D. (2021). Live presentation for eyewitness identification is not superior to photo or video presentation. *Journal of Applied Research in Memory and Cognition, 10*(1), 167–176.

Saks, M. J., & Koehler, J. J. (2005). The coming paradigm shift in forensic identification science. *Science, 309*(5736), 892–895.

Schweitzer, N. J., & Saks, M. J. (2007). The CSI effect: Popular fiction about forensic science affects the public's expectations about real forensic science. *Jurimetrics*, 357–364.

Smith, C. A. S., & Goodman, P. D. (1995). Forensic hair comparison analysis: Nineteenth century science or twentieth century snake oil. *Columbia Human Rights Law Review, 27*, 227.

Stenzel, C. (2016). Eyewitness misidentification: A mistake that blinds investigations, sways juries, and locks innocent people behind bars. *Creighton Law Review, 50*, 515.

The National Registry of Exonerations. (2024a). *% Exonerations by contributing factor*. https://www.law.umich.edu/special/exoneration/Pages/ExonerationsContribFactorsByCrime.aspx

The National Registry of Exonerations. (2024b). *The National Registry of exonerations 2023 annual report* (March 18, 2024). https://www.law.umich.edu/special/exoneration/Documents/2023%20Annual%20Report.pdf

Turvey, B. E. (2013). *Forensic fraud: Evaluating law enforcement and forensic science cultures in the context of examiner misconduct*.

Weinberg, M. (2021). *Juries, judges, and junk science-expert evidence on trial*. The Judicial Review: Selected Conference Papers: Journal of the Judicial Commission of New South Wales.

Wilson-Wilde, L., Smith, S., & Bruenisholz, E. (2017). The analysis of Australian proficiency test data over a ten-year period. *Forensic Science Policy & Management: An International Journal, 8*(1–2), 55–63.

Wilson-Wilde, L., Romano, H., & Smith, S. (2019). Error rates in proficiency testing in Australia. *Australian Journal of Forensic Sciences, 51*(supl), S268–S271.

Wixted, J. T., Wells, G. L., Loftus, E. F., & Garrett, B. L. (2021). Test a witness's memory of a suspect only once. *Psychological Science in the Public Interest, 22*(1_suppl), 1S–18S.

CHAPTER 7

Capability of Defendants: Navigating the Justice System

Abstract The next four chapters consider how the criminal justice system's structural limitations intersect with individuals' subjective lack of capability to create risk. This chapter examines how a defendant's subjective lack of capability—experience through cognitive and linguistic absence—can exclude them from meaningful participation in the criminal justice process. Despite formal safeguards, the justice system often operates on assumptions of competence that overlook the significant barriers faced by individuals who cannot understand, process, or communicate within legal contexts. The chapter explores how language deficits, cultural misunderstandings, and cognitive disabilities undermine defendants' rights, sometimes leading to false confessions or pleas, ineffective legal representation, and miscarriages of justice. The chapter further explores the fallibility of demeanour assessments and how misinterpretations can undermine credibility, especially for defendants from diverse linguistic and cultural backgrounds or with communication impairments. By analysing case studies like *Gibson and Murray v Feast*, alongside legal principles like the right to silence and the Anunga Rules, this book underscores the essential role of judicial gatekeeping in ensuring a fair trial for all, particularly vulnerable individuals. Ultimately, the chapter argues that access to justice demands not only procedural fairness but an active recognition of the capabilities required to engage with the system—and the profound consequences when those capabilities are lacking or ignored.

M. Ruyters et al., *Innocence Unveiled*,
https://doi.org/10.1007/978-3-031-91343-3_7

Keywords Wrongful conviction • Communication • Language barriers • Cognitive disadvantage • Fairness • Interpreters

A defendant's ability to communicate effectively, understand proceedings, and understand the impact of decisions that are offered to them to make is essential for access to justice and the right to a fair trial. There is often an assumption that individuals have the ability to navigate the criminal justice system despite clear barriers. This chapter examines the risks created through failures in understanding through language and cognitive disadvantages, a lack of English capacity, and misinterpretation of demeanour or silence. Language impairments, linguistic absence, and cognitive or intellectual disadvantages create significant barriers to adequate communication and can result in false confessions or false guilty pleas, which are addressed in Chap. 8.

Linguistic Absence

Linguistic presence is essential for a fair trial, ensuring that defendants can understand and express themselves through access to qualified interpreters (De Jongh, 2008; *Ebatarinja v Deland* (1998) 194 CLR 444, 454). Legal language is inherently complex, posing even greater challenges for people with limited English proficiency (Assy, 2011). The need for linguistic presence is particularly critical during police interviews, where misunderstandings can lead to false confessions. Ensuring linguistic presence, therefore, is an essential safeguard against potential miscarriages of justice.

The need for interpreters to ensure fair trials is well recognised in Australia (*Dietrich v The Queen* (1992) 177 CLR 292). The right to an interpreter in interviews with police and in legal proceedings is safeguarded in legislation. For instance, section 335 *Criminal Procedure Act 2009* (Vic) requires a competent interpreter if a person lacks sufficient English knowledge to understand proceedings, while section 464D(1) *Crimes Act 1958* (Vic) mandates delaying police questioning until an interpreter is present. Both provisions, however, require either the court or the police to make some assessment of the sufficiency of the person's English language knowledge. Australia's Uniform Evidence Acts ("UEA") provide that the police caution 'must be given in, or translated into, a language in which the person is able to communicate with reasonable fluency' (s139(3)), but this also requires an assessment of a defendant's "reasonable" English fluency. A failure to understand the police caution also does not, of itself, mean that an admission made during the interview was involuntary (*Luo v The Queen* [2020] WASCA 184).

The risk created by defendants' linguistic absence in Australia is substantial. In 2021, 3.4% (872,000) of Australia's population reported speaking English not well or not at all (Australian Bureau of Statistics "ABS", 2022). Of this group, 80.4% (702,000) were born overseas, with 59.2% having arrived in Australia earlier than 2011. Almost 77,000 Aboriginal and Torres Strait Islander peoples reported using 167 Aboriginal and Torres Strait Islander languages in 2021, and while 84.1% only spoke English at home, 9.5% spoke an Indigenous language at home (ABS, 2022). In the 2021 Census, 17% had reported not speaking English well or at all. Many Indigenous people also speak varieties of English which are different from General Australian English in "accent, grammar, word choice and meaning, pragmatics, discourse structure, and cultural presuppositions" (Eades, 2012, p. 474). For example, in *Murray v Feast* [2023] WASC 273, Murray, a Walmajarri man, successfully appealed his conviction for assault in the Magistrates' Court. Although he required an interpreter, the Magistrate instructed the interpreter not to interpret parts of Murray's testimony if it sounded like English, despite the interpreter explaining that Murray was speaking Aboriginal English and Kriol. On appeal, Solomon J found that the conduct of Murray's prosecution and conviction 'departed in a fundamental way from the requirements of fairness' ([171]). Setting aside Murray's conviction, Solomon J stated:

> The stark reality is this: a criminal prosecution of a Walmajarri man proceeded in the face of the court's express denial of the linguistic distinctiveness of the accused. Unintended though it was, this cannot be regarded as fair and just ([174]).

Solomon J explained that 'to deny the authenticity of a person's distinct linguistic identity or autonomy is to repudiate the authenticity of their cultural and perhaps spiritual essence; it is to impugn their sense of worth and value as a human being' ([171]).

Guidelines known as the "Anunga Rules" were established in 1976 to reduce disadvantages experienced by Indigenous accused (*R v Anunga* "Anunga" (1976) 11 ALR 412. The Rules include guidelines concerned with communication and language, which require that when an Indigenous person is interviewed by the police, an interpreter should be present where necessary, a 'prisoner's friend' should be present where practicable, care should be taken to ensure the person understands the police caution, and leading questions should be avoided (*Anunga,* p. 413). The rules have been applied or considered in other jurisdictions (e.g. WA, ACT and VIC), incorporated in part into police general orders (e.g. police general orders discussed in *The Queen v Bonson* [2019] NTSC 22 [41]) and applied to non-indigenous defendants (e.g. *Nguyen v The Queen* [2020] HCA 23 [76]). Notably, the court in *Anunga* recognised that the rules applied equally to the interrogation of migrants (p. 413). While the Anunga rules are not binding, they may be relevant in assessing whether a confession was provided voluntarily (Briggs & Scott, 2018, p. 30; *Western Australia v Gibson* (2014) 243 A Crim R [262], Hall J). Other safeguards are found in provisions such as section 464FA *Crimes Act 1958* (Vic), which provides that the Victoria Aboriginal Legal Service is to be notified if an Aboriginal person or a Torres Strait islander is taken into custody. Wrongful convictions occur, however, despite these efforts (Stratton & Sigamoney, 2020), as in the case of the Kiwirrkurra man Gene Gibson.

Gene Gibson

Gibson was initially interviewed in 2012 as a witness by police in relation to the death of Joshua Warneke. During the interview, which was not recorded, he made an admission about running down Warneke with a car (*The State of Western Australia v Gibson* "Gibson" [2014] WASC 240 [35]). He was then arrested, cautioned, and took part in a recorded interview during which he made a full confession. Gibson had lived most of his life in an isolated Aboriginal community. His first and second languages were Pintupi and Kukutja, and he only had a very basic understanding of English (*Gibson v The State of Western Australia* [2017] WASCA 141[10]–[11]). He was not provided with an interpreter for a second recorded interview nor provided with an interview friend (*Gibson,* 2014 [143]).

Gibson pleaded not guilty for murder, and the trial was set for August 2014. At a pre-trial hearing where the defence led to expert evidence from three linguists, Hall J held that the interviews were inadmissible. Hall J was not satisfied that Gibson's participation in the interviews was voluntary. Amongst other reasons, Gibson had not been cautioned in the first interview and did not understand the caution or his right to silence in the second. The interviews breached the *Criminal Investigation Act 2006* (WA) because of the failure to record the first interview and the failure to provide a qualified interpreter after Gibson's arrest. Hall J also held that it would be unfair to admit the interviews for reasons including that Gibson did not have the benefit of an independent interpreter, and there were doubts about the reliability of his answers in the interview due to his limited English (*Gibson,* 2014 [175]–[183]). Gibson's limited understanding of English, compounded by other factors, had placed him at a significant disadvantage (*The State of Western Australia v Gibson* [2014] WASC 240 [182]).

Gibson nonetheless went on to plead guilty to manslaughter. In 2017, his conviction was quashed by the Western Australia Court of Appeal. New expert evidence revealed Gibson's previously unknown significant cognitive impairment, which 'either alone or in combination with deficiencies in his linguistic capacity, deprived him of the ability to understand the nature of his plea of guilty and the implications of that plea' (*Gibson,* 2017 [65]–[77], [141]). The Court held that the integrity of his guilty plea was impugned by the likelihood that Gibson did not understand the legal process, the case against him, the advice of his defence lawyers, or the options that were available to him (*Gibson v The State of Western Australia* [2017] WASCA 141 [157). In addition to other factors including that he suffered from significant cognitive impairments, Gibson was unable to read written English or adequately understand or communicate in oral English in the context of his legal proceedings ([160]–[164]).

Judicial Gatekeeping

Gibson's case highlights the critical gatekeeping role of judges in evaluating the admissibility of confessional evidence. In 2024, we reviewed 21 Australian cases between 2001 and 2021 to understand how Australian judges perceived the English language proficiency of criminal defendants when assessing the admissibility of police interview evidence where language was an issue (Ruyters, Lai & Stratton, *forthcoming*). Judges relied on their own observations of recorded interviews noting factors such as defendants' vocabulary range, their use of 'understandable' English, and non-verbal engagement or responses. We found that when judges evaluated defendants' language competence during police interviews, they often assumed their own ability and epistemic competence to make decisions about matters which are typically reserved for experts and placed too much reliance on common sense to interpret complex cultural, linguistic, and behavioural nuances. Of the 21 cases, expert linguistic evidence was only received in *Gibson's* case.

The Australian Judicial Council on Cultural Diversity has developed national standards for working with interpreters, which recommend a four-part test ("JCDI test") for judges and lawyers to assess whether an interpreter is needed (Judicial Council, 2022). The absence of a court interpreter for defendants with limited English can lead to a miscarriage of justice (e.g. *R v Cruz* [2016] QCA 183; *R v Rostom* (2007) 98 SASR 528; but see *Nichols (a pseudonym v The Queen* [2021] VSCA 273). In *R v Rostom* (2007) 98 SASR 528, the Court of Criminal Appeal for South Australia held that a miscarriage of justice occurred where the trial judge had failed to ensure that a self-represented defendant had an opportunity to understand witness statements to be able to question them and conduct his defence. The majority held that the right to an interpreter during proceedings extends to the right of a defendant who does not speak English to have written evidence translated. Where a defendant is not represented, the judge must ensure that the defendant can read and consider written evidence in a language they understand (*Rostom*, 2007, p. 540 [47], [49] Gray and Sulan JJ).

Quality and Mode of Interpretation

Where interpreting is available, the quality of interpretation of the defendant's testimony matters, as this can have a substantial impact on juries' perceptions of the defendant's credibility as a witness (Hayes & Hale, 2010, p. 128), potentially leading to a miscarriage of justice (*James (a pseudonym) v The King* [2023] VSCA 34 [73]. In *R v Saraya* (1993) A Crim R 515, Mohammed Saraya was convicted of supplying heroin. His defence at trial was that he had taken possession of the heroin under duress. He gave evidence with the assistance of an interpreter, but a different interpreter was engaged in part of his cross-examination the following day. During his appeal, the court admitted expert evidence of deficiencies in the translation of questions posed by the Crown during the second day of cross-examination and of Saraya's responses. The Court of Appeal found that these deficiencies were significant enough to prevent Saraya from providing an accurate and effective account of facts essential to his defence. The court held that the right to an interpreter is fundamental to a fair trial if a defendant cannot adequately give evidence in English, and a conviction must be quashed if access to an interpreter is denied or the interpreting is inadequate (*Saraya,* 1993, p. 516).

However, even when interpreters are competent, defendants still face disadvantages. Defendants relying on interpreters are expected to retain everything communicated in court without any practical means of confirming the accuracy of the interpretation. As they are not provided with legal materials in their native language, they are entirely reliant on the interpreter's accuracy and their own ability to recall complex information. The mode of interpretation is another consideration. For instance, the interpreting mode of whispered simultaneous translation places the interpreter beside the defendant in the dock to relay what an English-speaking defendant would naturally understand, including witness testimony, legal arguments, and opposing counsel's objections (Hale et al., 2017, p. 77; Hale & Stern, 2011). This ongoing interpretation often occurs without access to materials, relying entirely on the interpreter's ability to convey meaning in real time. In *Makarov v The Queen (No. 2)* [2008] NSWCCA 292, however, the Court of Criminal Appeal held that the right to a fair trial did not extend to a requirement to provide simultaneous translation service (166]).

In addition to the challenges experienced by defendants, who are disadvantaged by their English language capacity, people with language and communication impairments face even greater difficulties as legal language often exceeds their ability to process and understand complex information.

Language Impairment

While legal language is challenging for most people, it is almost incomprehensible for people with language and communication impairments (Wszalek, 2017, p. 26). Language impairments refer to people's failure to acquire language usage and information processing competencies, particularly in oral communication skills such as listening and speaking which are typically developed from birth (LaVigne & Van Rybroek, 2013, p. 71; Snow & Powell, 2012, p. 1). In Australia, language impairment is a major concern, affecting an estimated 1.2 million people who face challenges in communication (ABS, 2015). Numerous studies have shown that people with speech and language disorders are disproportionately represented in the criminal justice system (see e.g. Henderson & Bull, 2024; Kippin et al., 2018; Maeve Dunn et al., 2023; LaVigne & Van Rybroek, 2013; Snow & Powell, 2011; Wszalek, 2017).

People with intellectual and developmental disabilities, such as developmental language disorder, face challenging communication barriers, making it difficult for them to understand the legal proceedings against them, let alone their rights (Ellem et al., 2022, p. 26). During interviews with police or meetings with defence lawyers, suspects are expected to answer complex questions, present information in a coherent narrative, and rationalise their states of mind, such as intention or decision-making (Holland et al., 2023). However, people with language impairments often have weak narrative skills, providing details about what happened but not explaining why events unfolded as they did (LaVigne & Van Rybroek, 2013, p. 89). There are also potential differences between written and oral communication abilities, which remain under-researched.

Language and communication barriers limit people's ability to understand information about their rights, with sometimes devastating effects. Research indicates, for instance, that a significant number of adults in the system struggle to understand the police caution (Chaulk et al., 2014; Pavlenko et al., 2019; Rendall & MacMahon, 2021). Defendants with disability may respond to incentives to plead guilty but not understand the consequences of doing so (Australian Human Rights Commission, 2014, p. 25; Marinos et al., 2017, p. 89). Despite these significant challenges, linguistic absence or impairments in oral language alone may not be sufficient to establish a miscarriage of justice. The case of Darry Beamish is an example of the challenges faced by people with communication barriers in the justice system.

Darryl Beamish was a young, deaf, non-verbal man with limited English who was convicted of a murder in 1961, notwithstanding evidence of potential police misconduct. Beamish was sentenced to death, although the sentence was later commuted to life imprisonment. His first appeal was dismissed in the same year. Despite serial killer Eric Edgar Cooke confessing to the murder in 1963, Beamish's second appeal following a petition of mercy was also refused. Two applications to the High Court and one to the Privy Council were also dismissed. Beamish was eventually released on parole in 1977. In 2002, the Western Australia Attorney General referred a new petition of mercy to the Western Australia Court of Appeal (*Beamish v The Queen* [2005] WASCA 62 [1]). In granting the appeal based on fresh evidence of Cooke's gallows confession, the Court observed that Beamish's poor communication skills 'might be thought to be a matter of some significance' for a reasonable jury ([419]–[420]). Beamish's frequent difficulties in communication were observable in the transcript of his evidence at the trial, and the court noted that his court-appointed interpreter was corrected by a check interpreter several times ([56]).

Some language impairments are attributable to cognitive or mental health impairments. In 2022, 39% of people entering Australian prisons disclosed a chronic condition or disability (Australian Institute of Health and Welfare (AIHS) 2022, p. 37; Dias et al., 2013). People with intellectual disabilities are also grossly over-represented in the corrections systems (Baldry et al., 2013; Hellenbach et al., 2017; VAGO, 2023). Indigenous Australians with disability, who are less likely to be identified as having disability than non-indigenous Australians, are also 14 times more likely than the general population to be imprisoned (AIHS, 2024, p. 248). People with intellectual disabilities are at increased risk of pleading guilty to crimes without fully understanding the plea process and are more susceptible to making false guilty pleas (Holt, 2024). Submissions to the Disability Royal Commission issues paper, for example, noted that people with disability might be incentivised to plead guilty to offences because of the threat of indefinite detention in the forensic mental health system (Royal Commission into Violence, 2023, p. 133).

The Significance of Silence: Right to Silence and Silent Defendants

Pressures to plead guilty can undercut the protections of the defendant's right to silence, as defendants may feel compelled to do what they can to secure their release or finalise their situation. Defendants have common law and statutory rights to remain silent pre-trial and at trial. The right to silence is supported by the caution requiring police to warn a suspect about their right to silence and the consequence of not exercising that right (see e.g. S 464A(3) *Crimes Act 1958* (Vic)) and statements taken by police will be taken to have been obtained improperly if the person was not cautioned before questioning begins (*UEA* s 139).

Silence protects defendants against self-incrimination, and generally, adverse inferences cannot be drawn from a defendant's choice to remain silent except where this is a fact in issue in the proceedings (e.g. *UEA* s 89). It is also desirable for the trial judge to warn the jury that the defendant's silence at trial is not evidence against them and should not be used to fill in gaps in the prosecution case (*Azzopardi v The Queen* (2001) 205 CLR 50; see also *Jury Directions Act 2015* (Vic) s 41). In *R v GAJ* [2011]

QCA 141, the trial judge did not give the jury any directions about the defendant's silence at his trial on sexual assault charges. The Queensland Court of Appeal allowed an appeal, holding that the failure to give the direction was a fundamental irregularity. The jury might have concluded that silence made it easier for them to accept the complainant's account, particularly when the trial judge had instructed them that their choice was 'really between the complainant's evidence and nothing' ([44]).

The right to silence is not absolute, however. Amendments were introduced in New South Wales in 2013, allowing juries to draw adverse inferences from a defendant's silence in proceedings for serious indictable offences if the defendant withheld information from police that they could reasonably have been expected to mention earlier, and which they later rely on in their defence (*Evidence Act 1995* (NSW) s89A). A special caution must first be given by police in the presence of a lawyer (Cameron, 2014; *Evidence Act* 1995 (NSW) s89A(2)), although this has created concerns that suspects may choose not to engage a lawyer during police questioning to circumvent the effect of section 89A (Daly, 2014, p. 71).

This dilution of the right to silence is part of other measures which have eroded the right to silence over the last couple of decades. For instance, section 39 of the *Major Crime (Investigative Powers) Act 2004* (Vic) abrogates the privilege against self-incrimination for witnesses summoned to appear before the Chief Examiner, who can compel witnesses to give evidence for the purpose of investigating organised crime offences. Compromising the protection of the right to remain silent is also aimed at increasing efficiencies (Cameron, 2014, p. 319; Gray, 2013, p. 163). Silent suspects mean that police may need to investigate other avenues to establish their case, increasing the complexity and resourcing of the investigation (Cameron, 2014, p. 319).

There is very little research on the impact of the right to silence, but there is some evidence to support a connection between lower conviction rates and asserting the right to silence (Leshem, 2010; Schofield-Georgeson, 2020). On the other hand, there is also research suggesting that jurors want or expect to hear from the defendant (Antonio & Arone, 2005; Bellin, 2017). Most defendants do not speak for themselves in court, which is commonly on the advice of their defence lawyers, and there are concerns that silent defendants are effectively denied participation in their cases, in effect being silenced by the people, entities, and structures that are put in place to protect them (Natapoff, 2005). In some cases, as we discuss below in the context of Mr. Big's confessions, defendants are not made aware they have the right to silence.

Credibility Assessments and Misinterpretation of Demeanour

Innocent defendants are also at risk of being misunderstood and misinterpreted through demeanour assessments. Despite the wide recognition that demeanour assessments are fallible, demeanour is still considered by juries and judges in assessing the credibility of witnesses, albeit with caution. Demeanour is 'intrinsically imprecise, including ephemeral expressions, hesitancy in speaking or responding, deliberate and involuntary actions and reactions, and manner of responding (*Gonzalez v The Queen* [2022] VSCA 41 [77]). Australian courts have an inconsistent approach to demeanour. While very cautious about the reliability of demeanour as an assessment of credibility or as an indication of guilt during police interviews, courts have relied on demeanour in considering a defendant's English language understanding in the same police interview context.

The credibility of witnesses is determined by the 'trier of fact', which is either the jury or the judge in judge-alone trials (*Farrell v The Queen* [1998] HCA 50 [27]). Judges may also assess credibility when considering, for example, expressions of remorse at sentencing (Rossmanith, 2015). Despite the importance placed on credibility assessments, however, they can be influenced by an apparently widely accepted pseudoscience belief that a person's demeanour or non-verbal behaviour reliably indicates their credibility (Denault & Bozin, 2024, p. 1; Qureshi, 2014; Smith, 2012, p. 34; Snook et al., 2017, p. 298). People constantly make instant assessments about the trustworthiness of strangers from their facial characteristics (Korva et al., 2013, p. 384), but assessments of credibility like this are inherently vulnerable to bias, particularly because of their dependence on intangibles. There are also acknowledged difficulties in assessing the credibility of witnesses from different cultural backgrounds (Alton, 2022, p. 28; *LH v The King* [2024] NSWCCA 165 [102]). Research suggests that facial evaluations, including "trustworthy" and "untrustworthy" faces and defendant's race impact leniency in sentencing and assessments of guilt (Korva et al., 2013, pp. 385, 395).

Recognising these vulnerabilities, Australian courts have tended to treat demeanour assessments cautiously. In *Fox v Percy* (2003) 214 CLR 118, Gleeson CJ, Gummow and Kirby JJ noted that judges were more aware of scientific research casting doubt on the ability of judges 'or anyone else' to tell if someone was lying from their appearance and of the danger in relying on appearance rather than objectively established facts (p. 129; *Pell v*

The Queen [2019] VSCA 186, [918]–[919], Weinberg JA). However, jurors may still be influenced by witnesses' appearance and demeanour. Chalmers et al. (2022, p. 399) found that jurors looked at the manner in which evidence was delivered as well as the content of the evidence and had expectations about how evidence should be delivered such as the extent to which complainants in sexual assault cases should be emotional when testifying. Jurors also looked for body language markers as signs of their false assumptions about that behaviour meant.

In Australia, directions are usually given to juries about the need to exercise care when considering demeanour (*R v Barrett* ([2007] VSCA 95; *LH v The Queen* [2024] NSWCCA 165). The case of *LH v the Queen* [2024] NSWCCA 165 is an example. The defendant was charged with child sexual assault offences in relation to his biological daughter. English was his second language, but he waived his right to an interpreter for the police interview. The Crown addressed the jury in the following terms:

> You might have thought that his reaction every time he learnt of a new allegation was totally unfazed, expressionless, emotionless. He didn't seem surprised at all. He didn't seem shocked at all. I'm not saying demeanour is everything and everybody is different, and everyone reacts different to different situations. ([82])

The trial judge then gave the following direction to the jury (102):

> In the Court's experience, it is well understood that even witnesses who are quite fluent in English as a second language can be disadvantaged when giving evidence in the formality of the courtroom.... There are difficulties in attempting to assess the truthfulness of a witness by reference to their body language or demeanour where different cultural backgrounds are involved and this problem may be exacerbated even more when evidence is given with the assistance of an interpreter.
>
> If a witness's answers appear to be unresponsive, incoherent or inconsistent and appear to lack candour, this may be due to the difficulty of interpreting concepts from one language to another. It is entirely a matter for you in the application of common sense as to what conclusions you draw in this regard.

Consciousness of Guilt

In rare cases, juries can also infer consciousness of guilt from their assessments of the defendant's demeanour in police interviews (*Ellis v The Queen*) [2010 VSCA 302 [41]; *LH v The King* [2024] NSWCCA 165 [188]; (*Favata* [2006] VSCA 44 [145], Vincent JA). In *R v Barrett* ([2007] VSCA 95 [31]–[32]), Eames JA said that these occasions would be rare 'having regard to the unreliability of demeanour as proof of the state of mind of any person, let alone as proof of guilt of a criminal offence. This should be accompanied by the direction to the jury on the use of demeanour, but a failure to give that direction does not necessarily mean there has been a miscarriage of justice' (*Ellis v The Queen*) [2010 VSCA 302 [41]).

Appeal courts will evaluate credibility assessments made by the jury or judge-alone in the context of the other evidence in the case. For example, in *Dansie v The Queen* [2020] SASCFC 103, Dansie was convicted of murdering his wife at a trial by judge-alone. Dansie was the primary caregiver for his wife, Helen, who had been reliant on a wheelchair for 22 years due to a stroke. While Dansie and his wife were alone, Helen's wheelchair entered a pond where she drowned. The evidence was circumstantial, but the prosecution case also relied on the financial and relationship motives. The trial judge observed that during his interview with the police, Dansie 'showed very little or no emotion that one might expect from a person who had just witnessed the death of his wife of many years.' Accepting the 'vagaries of human nature', the trial judge had regard to the other evidence in the case in assessing Dansie's personality (*Dansie,* 2020, [66]; *Pell v the Queen* [2020] HCA 12).

Research has shown that judges' initial assessment about a witness's trustworthiness based on demeanour can have a significant impact on how they interpret other information such as a defendant's expression of remorse (Porter & Ten Brinke, 2009; Porter et al., 2010, p. 10). As credibility assessments of witnesses are highly subjective and depend on intangible factors, they are susceptible to the influence of implicit bias (Alton, 2022, p. 46). For instance, in *Coombe v Bessell* [1994] TASSC 66, Coombe had been charged with assaulting his wife and causing property damage. Both Coombe and his wife testified, providing the main evidence in the case. The magistrate was clear in his reasons for deciding the complaint against Coombes that demeanour was of 'principal importance in determining credit' (*Coombe,* 1994, [5]). The magistrate was not aware, however, that Coombe had a speech impediment. On appeal, the Supreme Court of Tasmania found some of the ways in which the speech impediment manifested, such as a voice tremor, had led the magistrate to find that Coombe was not a credible witness (*Coombe,* 1994, [7]).

The assumption of competence in determining credibility by the Magistrate in *Coombe* reflects a broader judicial tendency to overestimate their capability and objectivity. In a 2024 study (Ruyters, Lai & Stratton, *forthcoming*), we found that several judges relied on their observations of defendants' demeanour and non-verbal cues in recorded video interviews to assess defendants' understanding of the caution and questioning (e.g. *State of Tasmania v Stojkovic* [2008] TASSC 48 [80]; *R v Deng* [2001] NSWCCA 153 [18]; *R v Lawrence* [2016 NTSC 65 [56]). It is problematic when judges rely on their assessment of demeanour to determine a person's language competence, particularly when assessing their linguistic competence in the language of the court.

A reliance on demeanour assessments, even with the safeguards of jury directions, poses a significant risk for wrongful convictions. While Australian courts recognise the fallibility of demeanour as an indicator of credibility or guilt, the risk of its influence persists. This reliance is a concern in contexts where implicit bias, cultural difference, potentially false assumptions about how language understanding is to be communicated, and other individual characteristics, such as Coombes' speech impediment, may skew juries' interpretations of behaviour. For instance, people with an undiagnosed autism spectrum disorder may present with characteristics that suggest untrustworthiness. In *The State of Western Australia v Mack* [2012] WASC 127, an autistic defendant, Brent Mack, was on trial for murdering his mother. In an affidavit in support of an application for trial by judge-alone, defence counsel described Mack's absence of eye contact, with his head remaining bowed, and 'the robotic manner in which he spoke'. McKechnie J, while discounting the likelihood that a properly instructed jury would draw adverse inferences from Mack's 'unusual personal characteristics', concluded that the interests of justice required a trial by judge-alone [4]. It is worth noting that there were 290,000 Autistic Australians in 2022, a 41.8% increase from 2018 (Australia Bureau of Statistics, 2022).

Legislation

Criminal Procedure Act 2009 (Vic)
Evidence Act 1995 (NSW)
Major Crime (Investigative Powers) Act 2004 (Vic)

Cases

Azzopardi v The Queen (2001) 205 CLR 50
Beamish v The Queen [2005] WASCA 62
Coombe v Bessell [1994] TASSC 66
Dansie v The Queen [2020] SASCFC 103
Dietrich v The Queen (1992) 177 CLR 292
Ebatarinja v Deland (1998) 194 CLR 444
Ellis v The Queen [2010] VSCA 302
Farrell v The Queen [1998] HCA 50
Favata [2006] VSCA 44
Fox v Percy (2003) 214 CLR 118
Gibson v The State of Western Australia [2017] WASCA 141
Gonzalez v The Queen [2022] VSCA 41
James (a pseudonym) v The King [2023] VSCA 34
LH v The Queen [2024] NSWCCA 165
Luo v The Queen [2020] WASCA 184
Makarov v The Queen (No. 2) [2008] NSWCCA 292
Maxwell v The Queen (1996) 184 CLR 501
Murray v Feast [2023] WASC 273
Nguyen v The Queen [2020] HCA 23
Nichols (a pseudonym v The Queen [2021] VSCA 273
Pell v The Queen [2019] VSCA 186
R v Anunga (1976) 11 ALR 412
R v *Barrett* ([2007] VSCA 95
R v Cruz [2016] QCA 183
R v Deng [2001] NSWCCA 153
R v GAJ [2011] QCA 141
R v Lawrence [2016 NTSC 65
R v Rostom (2007) 98 SASR 528
R v Saraya (1993) A Crim R 515
The Queen v Bonson [2019] NTSC 22
State of Tasmania v Stojkovic [2008] TASSC 48
The State of Western Australia v Gibson [2014] WASC 240
The State of Western Australia v Mack [2012] WASC 12
Western Australia v Gibson (2014) 243 A Crim R

References

Alton, M. A. (2022). The evolution of impartiality and the need for cultural competency when assessing credibility. *Canadian Journal of Administrative Law & Practice, 35*(1), 27–51.

Antonio, M. E., & Arone, N. E. (2005). Damned if they do, damned if they don't-jurors' reaction to defendant testimony or silence during a capital trial. *Judicature, 89*, 60.

Assy, R. (2011). Can the law speak directly to its subjects? The limitation of plain language. *Journal of Law and Society, 38*(3), 376–404.

Australia Bureau of Statistics. (2022). *2022 survey of disability, Ageing and Carers (SDAC) Autism in Australia*. In.

Australian Bureau of Statistics. (2015). *Disability, ageing and carers, Australia: Summary of findings*, 2015 (Catalogue No 4430.0,29 November 2017). https://www.abs.gov.au/statistics/health/disability/disability-ageing-and-carers-australia-summary-findings/latest-release.

Australian Bureau of Statistics. (2022). *Cultural Diversity: Census, 2021*. Retrieved 01/11/2024 from https://www.abs.gov.au/articles/cultural-diversity-australia#language

Australian Human Rights Commission. (2014). *Equal before the law: Towards disability justice strategies*. Australian Human Rights Commission. https://humanrights.gov.au/sites/default/files/document/publication/2014_Equal_Before_the_Law.pdf

Australian Institute of Health and Welfare ("AIHS"). (2022). *The health of people in Australia's prisons*. https://www.aihw.gov.au/getmedia/e2245d01-07d1-4b8d-81b3-60d14fbf007f/aihw-phe-33-health-of-people-in-australias-prisons-2022.pdf?v=20231108163318&inline=true

Australian Institute of Health and Welfare ("AIHS"). (2024). *People with disability in Australia 2024*. https://www.aihw.gov.au/getmedia/725731a5-5296-4b8d-8e49-40fa64937fb2/aihw-dis-72-people-with-disability-in-australia-2024.pdf?v=20240403105922&inline=true

Baldry, E., Clarence, M., Dowse, L., & Trollor, J. (2013). Reducing vulnerability to harm in adults with cognitive disabilities in the Australian criminal justice system. *Journal of Policy and Practice in Intellectual Disabilities, 10*(3), 222–229.

Bellin, J. (2017). The silence penalty. *Iowa Law Review, 103*, 395.

Briggs, J., & Scott, R. (2018). Police interviews and coerced false confessions: Gibson v Western Australia (2017) 51 WAR 199. *Journal of Judicial Administration, 28*(1), 22–43.

Cameron, A. (2014). Common sense or unnecessary complexity: The recent change to the right to silence in New South Wales. *Deakin Law Review, 19*, 311.

Chalmers, J., Leverick, F., & Munro, V. E. (2022). Handle with care: Jury deliberation and demeanour-based assessments of witness credibility. *The International Journal of Evidence & Proof, 26*(4), 381–406.

Chaulk, S. J., Eastwood, J., & Snook, B. (2014). Measuring and predicting police caution comprehension in adult offenders. *Canadian Journal of Criminology and Criminal Justice, 56*(3), 323–340.

Daly, Y. M. (2014). The right to silence: Inferences and interference. *Australian & New Zealand Journal of Criminology, 47*(1), 59–80.

De Jongh, E. M. (2008). Court interpreting: Linguistic presence v. linguistic absence. *Florida Bar Journal, 82*(7), 20.

Denault, V., & Bozin, D. (2024). The influence of "body language" on the assessment of witness credibility in Australian written court judgments. *Journal of Forensic Psychology Research and Practice*, 1–17.

Dias, S., Ware, R. S., Kinner, S. A., & Lennox, N. G. (2013). Co-occurring mental disorder and intellectual disability in a large sample of Australian prisoners. *Australian & New Zealand Journal of Psychiatry, 47*(10), 938–944.

Eades, D. (2012). Communication with aboriginal speakers of English in the legal process. *Australian Journal of Linguistics, 32*(4), 473–489.

Ellem, K., Dowse, L., Rowe, S., Holland, L., Cullin, J., Parker, M., & Henderson, C. (2022). *Insights from people with lived experience of disability and the justice system*. The University of Queensland.

Gray, A. (2013). Constitutionally heeding the right to silence in Australia. *Monash University Law Review, 39*(1), 156–187.

Hale, S., & Stern, L. (2011). Interpreter quality and working conditions: Comparing Australian and international courts of justice. *Judicial Officers Bulletin, 23*(9), 1–4.

Hale, S., Martschuk, N., Ozolins, U., & Stern, L. (2017). The effect of interpreting modes on witness credibility assessments. *Interpreting, 19*(1), 69–96.

Hayes, A., & Hale, S. (2010). Appeals on incompetent interpreting. *Journal of Judicial Administration, 20*(2), 119–130.

Hellenbach, M., Karatzias, T., & Brown, M. (2017). Intellectual disabilities among prisoners: Prevalence and mental and physical health comorbidities. *Journal of Applied Research in Intellectual Disabilities, 30*(2), 230–241.

Henderson, C. A., & Bull, M. (2024). Sentencing and the over-representation of people with cognitive disability in the Australian criminal justice system. *Current Issues in Criminal Justice, 36*(1), 81–98.

Holland, C., Hutchinson, P., & Peacock, D. (2023). The importance of screening for speech, language and communication needs (SLCN) in police custody. *The Howard Journal of Crime and Justice, 62*(3), 295–312.

Holt, G. A. (2024). Reducing the risk of false guilty pleas: How has the disability Royal Commission addressed this pathway to wrongful conviction for people with intellectual disabilities? *Research and Practice in Intellectual and Developmental Disabilities, 11*(2), 265–277.

Kippin, N. R., Leitão, S., Watkins, R., Finlay-Jones, A., Condon, C., Marriott, R., Bower, C., et al. (2018). Language diversity, language disorder, and fetal alcohol spectrum disorder among youth sentenced to detention in Western Australia. *International Journal of Law and Psychiatry, 61*, 40–49.

Korva, N., Porter, S., O'Connor, B. P., Shaw, J., Brinke, L., & t. (2013). Dangerous decisions: Influence of juror attitudes and defendant appearance on legal decision-making. *Psychiatry, Psychology and Law, 20*(3), 384–398.

LaVigne, M., & Van Rybroek, G. (2013). "He got in my face so I shot him": How defendants' language impairments impair attorney-client relationships. *The City University of New York (CUNY) Law Review, 17*, 69.

Leshem, S. (2010). The benefits of a right to silence for the innocent. *The Rand Journal of Economics, 41*(2), 398–416.

Maeve Dunn, L., Symkovych, A., & Johns, D. (2023). The gendered framing of language impairments in criminalised young people. *Criminology & Criminal Justice, 17488958231193128.*

Marinos, V., Griffiths, D., Robinson, J., Gosse, L., Fergus, C., Stromski, S., & Rondeau, K. (2017). Persons with intellectual disabilities and the criminal justice system: A view from criminal justice professionals in Ontario. *Criminal Law Quarterly, 64*, 83.

Natapoff, A. (2005). Speechless: The silencing of criminal defendants. *New York University Law Review, 80*, 1449.

Pavlenko, A., Hepford, E., & Jarvis, S. (2019). An illusion of understanding: How native and non-native speakers of English understand (and misunderstand) their Miranda rights. *International Journal of Speech Language and the Law, 26*(2).

Porter, S., & Ten Brinke, L. (2009). Dangerous decisions: A theoretical framework for understanding how judges assess credibility in the courtroom. *Legal and Criminological Psychology, 14*(1), 119–134.

Porter, S., Ten Brinke, L., & Gustaw, C. (2010). Dangerous decisions: The impact of first impressions of trustworthiness on the evaluation of legal evidence and defendant culpability. *Psychology, Crime & Law, 16*(6), 477–491.

Qureshi, A. M. (2014). Relying on demeanour evidence to assess credibility during trial: A critical examination. *Criminal Law Quarterly, 61*, 235.

Rendall, M., & MacMahon, K. (2021). Influences on understanding of a verbally presented police caution amongst adults involved in the criminal justice system: a systematic review. *Psychiatry, Psychology and Law, 28*(1), 70–93.

Rossmanith, K. (2015). Affect and the judicial assessment of offenders: Feeling and judging remorse. *Body & Society, 21*(2), 167–193.

Royal Commission into Violence, A Neglect and Exploitation of People with Disability. (2023). *Final Report - Volume 8, Criminal justice and people with disability.* https://disability.royalcommission.gov.au/system/files/2023-09/Final%20Report%20-%20Volume%208%2C%20Criminal%20justice%20and%20people%20with%20disability.pdf

Schofield-Georgeson, E. (2020). Silence matters: A survey of the right to silence in the summary jurisdiction of New South Wales. *The International Journal of Evidence & Proof, 24*(2), 121–141.

Smith, L. (2012). The ring of truth, the clang of lies: Assessing credibility in the courtroom. *UNBLJ, 63*, 10.

Snook, B., McCardle, M. I., Fahmy, W., & House, J. C. (2017). Assessing truthfulness on the witness stand: Eradicating deeply rooted pseudoscientific beliefs about credibility assessment by triers of fact. *Canadian Criminal Law Review, 22*(3), 297–306.

Snow, P. C., & Powell, M. B. (2011). Oral language competence in incarcerated young offenders: Links with offending severity. *International Journal of Speech-Language Pathology, 13*(6), 480–489.

Snow, P., & Powell, M. (2012). Youth (in) justice: Oral language competence in early life and risk for engagement in antisocial behaviour in adolescence. *Trends and Issues in Crime and Criminal Justice, 435*, 1–6.

Stratton, G., & Sigamoney, A. (2020). Why we Don't see race: How Australia has overlooked race as an influence on miscarriages of justice. *Race and Justice*, 2153368720922294.

Victorian Auditor-General's Office. (VAGO). (2023). *Correctional services for people with intellectual disability or an acquired brain injury*. V. A.-G. s. office. https://www.audit.vic.gov.au/sites/default/files/2023-06/20230622_Correctional-Services-Intellectual%20Disability-or-an-ABI.pdf?

Wszalek, J. (2017). Ethical and legal concerns associated with the comprehension of legal language and concepts. *AJOB Neuroscience, 8*(1), 26–36.

CHAPTER 8

The Problem of Confessional Evidence: False Guilty Pleas and Plea Negotiations

Abstract This chapter examines how the phenomena of false guilty pleas and false confessions present a potential barrier to achieving justice in Australia. We highlight how the combination of communication barriers and systemic incentives contributes to a high rate of guilty pleas and reflect on systemic incentives such as sentencing discounts for early pleas and prosecution performance indicators that encourage plea negotiations. We consider how systemic pressures—aggravated by punitive justice policies, restrictive bail laws, and coercive police practices—can lead innocent individuals to plead guilty or falsely confess. The chapter presents the drivers of false confessions as significant risks, such as police interviewing practices, communication barriers, institutionalised racism, and individual vulnerabilities, and considers the challenges of appealing convictions based on guilty pleas or confessions.

Keywords Wrongful convictions • False guilty pleas • False confessions • Plea negotiations • Systemic incentives • Vulnerable individuals

Communication barriers significantly impact defendants' decision making, increasing their susceptibility to making false guilty pleas and false confessions. In Australia, most criminal cases are resolved through guilty pleas, usually negotiated between the defence and prosecution. Early guilty pleas

M. Ruyters et al., *Innocence Unveiled*,
https://doi.org/10.1007/978-3-031-91343-3_8

are encouraged through systemic incentives, including sentencing discounts offered by legislatures and courts, and prosecution bodies reporting guilty outcomes as key performance indicators. Innocent guilty pleas highlight deeper systemic issues, including punitive justice policies. There are also structural incentives to secure confessions when these are needed to strengthen cases that rely on weak circumstantial evidence. These can lead to confessions obtained through the sanctioned use of deception and inducements in police operations or misconduct in some cases. The risk of wrongful convictions is aggravated when structural and systemic aims combine with vulnerabilities, such as mental health issues, cognitive impairment, lack of understanding, race, or gender.

False Guilty Pleas and Plea Negotiations

In Australia, most criminal cases are resolved through an acknowledgement of guilt (Australian Bureau of Statistics "ABS", 2023), with research suggesting that between 80% and 100% of guilty pleas result from plea negotiations (Flynn & Freiberg, 2018). Plea negotiations, often referred to as plea bargains, charge bargains, state-induced guilty pleas, negotiated resolutions, or appropriate early resolutions, involve discussions between the defence and prosecution about an accused person's likely plea (Flynn & Freiberg, 2018; McConville & Marsh, 2014). These discussions can involve negotiating the charges, facts of the case, and the prosecution's sentencing submission, with the aim of arriving at an agreement where the accused pleads guilty (Flynn, 2011).

There is no official data collected about plea negotiations in Australia (Flynn, 2016; Flynn & Freiberg, 2018); however, data released by prosecution bodies give some indication. Incentives towards guilty pleas are built into the prosecution process. Prosecution bodies report on guilty outcomes as measures of performance against targets (e.g. OPP, 2023, p. 91), while early guilty pleas are emphasised as efficiencies such as the Early Appropriate Guilty Plea (EAGP) reform package introduced in New South Wales in 2018 to encourage early appropriate guilty pleas in indictable proceedings (Trimboli, 2021) and in prosecution annual reports (NSWODPP, 2023, p. 30). The EAGP reforms incentivise guilty pleas through sentencing discounts, providing a 25% discount for a guilty plea prior to committal and discounts which decrease incrementally after the committal (*Crimes (Sentencing Procedure) Act 1999* (NSW) section 25D).

It is not clear whether prosecution guilty plea statistics include Indigenous defendants who pleaded guilty as a condition of eligibility for entry into Koori Courts.

Innocent Guilty Pleas

There is increasing recognition that innocent individuals plead guilty to crimes they did not commit (National Registry of Exonerations; Roach, 2021). In England and Wales, almost 40% of cases referred to the Court of Appeal by the Criminal Cases Review Commission since 2012 involved defendants who initially pleaded guilty (Helm, 2019). A 2024 Australian study of appellate court judgements where a guilty plea conviction was overturned has also found more than 200 factual, legal, and procedural errors contributing to the wrongful convictions (Nash et al., 2024). The study did not examine the role of plea negotiations, highlighting a general tendency to exclude plea negotiations from wrongful conviction considerations (Roach, 2021).

When accepting a guilty plea, courts must be satisfied that the defendant made the decision voluntarily, free of any undue pressure or coercion (Roach Anleu & Mack 2009). This principle is well-documented in *Maxwell v The Queen* (1996) 184 CLR 501, where the High Court held that a guilty plea must be unequivocal and not made under circumstances suggesting it is not a genuine admission of guilt. Numerous Australian and international studies have found, however, that defendants enter plea negotiations and guilty pleas for reasons other than accepting guilt, with various psychological, social, and structural pressures potentially influencing their decision (Hussemann & Siegel, 2018; Moffa et al., 2024; Redlich et al., 2017). These pressures can include financial constraints (Peterson, 2019), a desire to protect others (Jones, 2011; Roach Anleu & Mack, 2009), intimidation from others (*Meissner v The Queen* (1995) 184 CLR 132, p. 157, Dawson J), coercion or pressure from defence lawyers (Baldwin & McConville, 1977; Nash et al., 2024), lack of understanding about the nature of a guilty plea (e.g. *Gibson v The State of Western Australia* [2017] WASCA 141) or a wish to resolve the case as efficiently as possible (Mack & Roach Anleu, 1995). Defendants may also misunderstand or misinterpret advice from defence lawyers (see comments in *Hogue v The State of Western Australia* [2005] WASCA 102 [35], Wheeler JA for the court).

The pressure to plead guilty may be heightened for more minor, summary offences, where a cost–benefit analysis may be more pronounced (Cheng, 2013; Betley, 2024; Duce, 2024; Roach, 2021). Further, vulnerable individuals, such as those with cognitive impairments, mental health concerns, young people, Indigenous and other racialised accused, and women, are particularly susceptible to system pressures and may be more likely to enter a false guilty plea [Schehr & French, 2015)].

Cognitive disabilities add a significant layer of vulnerability in plea decisions. Nash's et al. (2024) study, for example, identified 14 cases in which cognitive impairment or mental illness prevented individuals from understanding the legal process, charges, or consequences of their guilty plea. Legal practitioners have reported substantial challenges in communicating with clients who have impairments, including difficulties in giving and receiving instructions and ensuring the client understood the gravity of the plea (Flynn & Freiberg, 2018; Lansdell et al., 2021). Fear of subjecting defendants to indefinite detention has led to defendants with cognitive impairments being "pleaded up" to expedite the process contributing to wrongful convictions among a highly vulnerable population (Holt, 2024). Addressing the problem of false guilty pleas is crucial to reducing the overrepresentation of incarcerated people with cognitive disabilities, particularly amongst Indigenous peoples (Baldry et al., 2013; Carling, 2017). As Carling (2017, p. 420) emphasised, 'those working in the criminal justice system looking to reduce the overrepresentation of Indigenous people ought to be particularly concerned about the various reasons Indigenous accused plead out.' Gene Gibson's case is a stark example of this risk.

Appeals against conviction where a defendant has pleaded guilty are difficult and will only be successful in exceptional circumstances (*Arkeveld v Director of Public Prosecutions* [2023] WASC 264 [41], Lundberg J; see, however, *R v D'Orta-Ekenaike* [1998] 2 VR 140). The defendant will need to establish circumstances that amount to a miscarriage of justice (*Hogue v The State of Western Australia* "Hogue" [2005] WASCA 102 [22], Wheeler JA, with Malcolm CJ and Le Miere AJA in agreement). While not exhaustive, recognised circumstances are where the defendant did not understand the nature of the charge, such as in Gibson's case or did not intend to admit guilty, and where the guilty plea was obtained by improper inducement, fraud, or intimidation (*Hogue* [22]; *Snook v The State of Western Australia* [2015] WASCA 29 [102], Hall J with Buss and Mazza JJA in agreement). But it will not be enough that evidence on the appeal might show that the appellant was not guilty of the offence—it must also be shown that there was a miscarriage of justice (*Meissner v The Queen* (1995) 184 CLR 132 [19], Dawson J). Tammy Lysaght's case, however, illustrates that a finding of a miscarriage of justice does not necessarily address social and structural determinants of inequality in the justice system.

Tammy Louise Lysaght was wrongly convicted in 2011 for the aggravated unlawful assault of her 16-month-old daughter and sentenced to sentenced to one year imprisonment, suspended for one year. Lysaght denied any wrongdoing. In 2016, police became aware that Lysaght's partner, Robert Dacey, had admitted to assaulting the child but threatened to kill Lysaght and her family if she reported him (*Lysaght v Youlden* [2018] WASC 38). In a statement to police, Lysaght said that despite her instructions to her lawyer that she did not assault her daughter and that she wished to plead not guilty, she was advised to plead guilty to avoid immediate imprisonment and that it would be viewed favourably by the child protection agency. She stated: 'I felt pressured by the lawyer to plead guilty because he suggested if I didn't I would go to jail for a very long time' [*Lysaght,* [20], Jenkins J). Dacey was subsequently convicted of an assault in 2017. Lysaght then successfully appealed to her conviction in 2017 on the fresh evidence of Dacey's admissions (*Lysaght,* 2018). Despite acknowledging the miscarriage of justice, Jenkins J refused Lysaght's application for appeal costs, stating that her decision to plead guilty was unreasonable as she had deliberately led the police and court to believe she was responsible. He stated, 'It does not seem to me that this is a situation in which the system has failed the appellant or a situation in which the respondent failed the appellant' ([44]). This case highlights gender-specific pressures on women to plead guilty, including threats from abusive relationships and childcare concerns (Jones, 2011), and poor judicial understandings of family violence dynamics and their impact on women's plea decisions (see Moffa et al., 2024).

The Influence of Punitive Policies

Pressures on innocent accused persons to enter false guilty pleas in Australia are situated within a broader context of systemic issues in the criminal justice system. This environment is shaped by increasingly punitive "tough on crime" policies, which have aggravated legal needs and further restricted access to justice for many who were already having difficulties, including Indigenous Australians, homeless individuals, women, and people with disabilities (Law Council of Australia, 2018; Corpuz et al., 2022). Punitive policies governing bail, mandatory minimum sentences, and managerialist approaches to lower-level summary offences have created potentially insuperable pressures on innocent people to plead guilty. In the United States, discussions around bail policy and wrongful convictions often highlight the disproportionate impact of bail policies on low-income individuals who cannot afford bail, resulting in a higher rate of wrongful convictions among economically disadvantaged groups (see, e.g. Mansoor, 2020; Wiseman, 2016). Australian jurisdictions tend not to operate on a cash-bail system, but several jurisdictions have undergone significant bail policy reform, which have restricted access to bail and increased the number of unsentenced prisoners.

The unintended consequences of bail reform are illustrated in the suite of reforms introduced in 2017 after James Gargasoulas used his car to kill six people and injure many others (Wright, 2023, p. 5; *DPP v Gargasoulas* [2019] VSC 87). The tragic event prompted the Victorian government to quickly enact a sweep of bail policy changes with the aim of preventing repeat offenders from obtaining bail (Wright, 2023, pp. 5–6). Amendments to the *Bail Act* 1977 (Vic) retained a presumption in favour of bail in section 4, but expanded the number of offences to which reverse onus tests would apply, creating a presumption against bail for those offences (McMahon, 2019, p. 14).The reverse onus tests require an accused person to establish exceptional circumstances or compelling reasons why they should be released on bail (*Bail Act 1977* ss 4A, 4C). The amendments had significant implications for criminalised women, who faced multiple forms of disadvantages relevant to bail applications, such as limited access to housing, a lack of personal relationships and family support, poor mental health, and alcohol and drug abuse (Russell et al., 2020). Research exploring the drivers of women's increasing rates of remand in Victoria has found that high bail thresholds can create pressure on women to plead out their matters (Russell et al., 2020). In 2023, the coroner in the inquiry into Gunditjmara, Dja Dja Wurrung, Wiradjuri, and Yorta Yorta woman Veronica Nelson's death in custody in 2020 also emphasised the likely impact of bail policy on plea decisions, stating, '[t]he provisions incentivise a plea of guilty to avoid time in custody where the prospects of bail are limited. *A guilty plea is the more direct route to freedom* (McGregor, 2023, p. 132, emphasis added).

False Confessions

The concept of an innocent person falsely confessing to a crime they did not commit is difficult to comprehend. Yet, it is a frequent phenomenon. In the United States, 12% of recorded exonerations involved a false confession, a figure that rises to 69% when considering the causal factors of homicide wrongful convictions (National Registry of Exonerations, 2024). In Australia, the issue of false confessions is equally concerning despite being under-researched (McQuire, 2019). According to a 2015 study, approximately 17% of recorded wrongful convictions in Australia have involved a false confession (Dioso-Villa, 2015). There appear to be two significant drivers for potential false confessions in Australia: police interviewing practices leading to coerced or fabricated confessions and race, which are discussed next. We would also include the induced confessions resulting from Mr. Big scenario operations, which are discussed in Chap. 11 because police target suspects who are psychologically predisposed to responding to pressure, for instance, because of mental illness, financial need, or low self-esteem (Iftene & Kinnear, 2020, pp. 301–302).

False confessions appear to be widespread in wrongful convictions experienced by Indigenous people, including in Australia (Roach, 2015, p. 243). Roach suggested that false confessions may be symptomatic of deeper issues of racial bias and racist tunnel vision, police violence against Indigenous suspects, and suspects' despair about their ability to prove they are innocent (2015, p. 243). Van Buuren (2024) highlighted a persistent and ongoing lack of availability, and limited use, of interpreters at different stages in the justice process. In some cases, this inadequacy has contributed to significant miscarriages of justice, such as in Gene Gibson's case, where police denied Gibson access to an interpreter despite his primary language being Pintupi. Gibson was unable to understand his legal rights or the questions the police put to him, leading him to his false murder confession (*Gibson v The State of Western Australia* [2017] WASCA 141 [157]; van Buuren, 2024, pp. 194–195). Gibson told his lawyer the reason he made the confession was because the police were not listening to him and 'nobody else was listening to him' [2017] WASCA 141 [122].

Andrew Mallard's case is a recognised wrongful conviction case resulting, in part, from false confessions which the Western Australia Corruption and Crime Commission ("CCC") considered to be due to the mental illness Mallard was suffering at the time (CCC, 2008, p. xxvi). (xxvi). Pamela Lawrence was murdered in her shop on 23 May 1994. The following day,

Mallard was arrested on unrelated charges and remanded for psychiatric assessment until 10 June 1991. He was interviewed on four occasions while he was there about Mrs. Lawrence's death where he provided unsupported alibis. On 10 June, Mallard was taken to the police station where he was questioned for over eight hours without first being cautioned or charged. Then on 17 June, he was interviewed again for three hours despite police being aware he had had little sleep the night before. Both interviews were unrecorded, and the questions and answers were manually recorded by the police. 17 June interview was followed by a short 30-minute video recorded interview. During the unrecorded interview on 17 June Mallard made a series of contradictory admissions, providing a description of the murder weapon and what had happened, and then denying any involvement (*Mallard v The Queen* (2005) 224 CLR 125, pp. 132–138; Corruption and Crime Commission, 2008, pp. xvii–xix). While recording equipment was clearly available and there were guidelines about the desirability of recording in serious cases, the practice at the time was to only video record interview when a suspect had made admissions (CCC, 2008; *Mallard v The Queen,* SLR, unreported, P 52/1996, 24 October 1997, [22], Malcolm CJ).

After a petition for clemency was filed on Mallard's behalf, it emerged that the police and prosecution had withheld key evidence from the defence that contradicted their narrative, including the fact that police had unsuccessfully attempted to replicate Lawrence's wounds by striking a pig's head with a wrench. The police also failed to disclose to the prosecution that they had required a forensic expert to remove critical information and altered other witnesses' statements to exclude content favourable to Mallard. Mallard's conviction was later quashed by the High Court in 2005. Mallard's case led to reforms in Western Australia's laws regarding the recording of admissions. Section 118 of the *Criminal Investigation Act* 2006 (WA) now states that admissions in serious cases are inadmissible if not recorded, unless there is a reasonable excuse for not doing so or the court otherwise decides.

Fabricated Confessions: The Art of "Verballing"

Australian police forces have a long history with the practice of "verballing", which is false evidence given by police about a confession (Dixon, 2006; Durnian, 2020). Verballing occurred from at least the 1960s and likely earlier (Alderson, 2001, pp. 253, 257). While it is difficult to estimate its extent, a study found that in 96.6% of cases in NSW in the early 1980s, for example, defendants confessed or made admissions during police interviews (Stevenson, 1982, p. 132). Verballing continued to the early 2000s by which time requirements for audio-visual recorded interviews were becoming common across Australia (Alderson, 2001, p. 280). Police verballing practices were exposed through numerous Commissions and inquiries (e.g. Beach, 1976; Lucas, 1977; Wood, 1997) with the Wood Royal Commissioner describing verballing as a 'form of art' (Wood, 1997, p. 76). Verballing was rife in the 1980s, featuring in the New South Wales Police Integrity Commission' Operation Florida, which reviewed corruption across the 1980s to early 2000s (New South Wales Police Integrity Commission, 2004). An example of this occurred in the case of the Mickelberg brothers, where the 1983 convictions of Ray and Peter Mickelberg for offences relating to a conspiracy to defraud the Perth Mint were quashed in 2004 after one of the detectives investigating the case admitted to fabricating confessional statements and committing perjury (*Mickelberg v The Queen* ("*Mickelberg*") [2004] WASCA 145).

In addition to requirements to electronically record evidence of an admission such as section 464H of the *Crimes Act 1958 (Vic)*, legislative protections were introduced, excluding documentary evidence of alleged admissions such as police notes unless the defendant acknowledged the document as a true record (see e.g. *Uniform Evidence Acts*, s86: *McKinney v The Queen* (1991) 191 CLR 468). While these do not exclude the possibility of verballing, as police can still give oral evidence about alleged admissions, including those that are alleged to have been made outside the recorded interview, further protection is available through jury directions on unreliable evidence. Unsupported evidence of an admission, for instance, where the admission was not recorded, will attract a direction to the jury about the matters that might cause the admission to be unreliable and the need for caution in accepting the evidence (e.g. *Jury Directions Act 2015* (Vic) ss 31, 32). Note that the term "admission" is being used here as an umbrella term for admissions and confessions when referring to Australian legislation.

Coerced and Induced Confessions

These protections, however, do not really address the type of investigative techniques used by the police. Following injustices linked to coercive interviewing techniques used by police, Australia and several other countries reformed their interviewing practices, shifting their focus from obtaining confessions to gathering information in most cases (Adam & van Golde, 2020; Howes, 2020; Stratton & Moffa, 2023). The implementation, training, and use of the PEACE interview strategy in Australia, which varies by jurisdiction, is unclear, however, due to limited public access to resources such as training manuals or procedural guidelines for police interviews (Adam & van Golde, 2020).

While there are protections against coerced, induced, and unsupported confessions obtained during official questioning (see, e.g. *Uniform Evidence Acts* ss 84–86), Australian law enforcement agencies are free to use covert methods to induce confessions following the decision of the High Court in *Tofilau v The Queen* (2007) 231 CLR 396). The High Court upheld the admissibility of confessions obtained through the Mr. Big scenario technique despite the deception inherent in the methodology. Mr. Big scenario operations are aimed to induce or elicit confessions from a suspect and have been used by Australian law enforcement since the 1990s (Ruyters & Bartle, 2024). This technique, which we discuss in more detail in Chap. 10, bypasses several protective factors used in interviewing suspects, such as the right to silence or the right to a legal representative. While there have been no recorded wrongful convictions arising from Mr. Big operations in Australia, the practice is internationally recognised as risking the production of false confessions and wrongful convictions (Ruyters & Bartle, 2024; Adam & van Golde, 2024).

False confessions are a significant issue not only because they produce inaccurate or misleading evidence but also because they may encourage the innocent defendant to plead guilty. According to research in the United States, an exoneree who previously gave a false confession is over three times more likely to enter a false guilty plea compared to one who never confessed, as they often feel they have little chance of being believed by a jury (National Registry of Exoneration, 2015). Overturning false confession convictions is also challenging (Gross & O'Brien, 2008).

Legislation

Bail Act 1977 (Vic)
Crimes Act 1958 (Vic)
Crimes (Sentencing Procedure) Act 1999 (NSW)
Criminal Investigation Act 2006 (WA)
Jury Directions Act 2015 (Vic)

Uniform Evidence Acts

Cases

Arkeveld v Director of Public Prosecutions [2023] WASC 264
DPP v Gargasoulas [2019] VSC 87
Gibson v The State of Western Australia [2017] WASCA 141
Hogue v The State of Western Australia [2005] WASCA 102
Lysaght v Youlden [2018] WASC 38
McKinney v The Queen (1991)
Mallard v The Queen (2005) 224 CLR 125
Mallard v The Queen, SLR, unreported, P 52/1996, 24 October 1997
Meissner v The Queen (1995) 184 CLR 132
R v D'Orta-Ekenaike [1998] 2 VR 140
Snook v The State of Western Australia [2015] WASCA 29
Tofilau v The Queen (2007) 231 CLR 396

References

Adam, L., & van Golde, C. (2020). Police practice and false confessions: A search for the implementation of investigative interviewing in Australia. *Alternative Law Journal, 45*(1), 52–59.

Adam, L., & van Golde, C. (2024). Is it time to move on from 'Mr Big'? Scenario evidence and the risk of unreliable confessions in Australia. *Alternative Law Journal, 49*(2), 134–141.

Alderson, K. (2001). *Powers and responsibilities: Reforming NSW criminal investigation law* UNSW Sydney].

Baldry, E., Clarence, M., Dowse, L., & Trollor, J. (2013). Reducing vulnerability to harm in adults with cognitive disabilities in the Australian criminal justice system. *Journal of Policy and practice in Intellectual Disabilities, 10*(3), 222–229.

Baldwin, J., & McConville, M. (1977). *Negotiated justice: Pressures to plead guilty.* Martin Robertson.

Betley, P. (2024). Pleading for justice: Analyzing Ohio's wrongful conviction compensation statute and the guilty plea disqualification provision. *Cleveland State University College of Law, 72*(3), 753–780.

Carling, A. (2017). A way to reduce indigenous overrepresentation: Prevent false guilty plea wrongful convictions. *Criminal Law Quarterly, 64,* 415.

Cheng, K. K.-Y. (2013). Pressures to plead guilty: Factors affecting plea decisions in Hong Kong's magistrates' courts. *British Journal of Criminology, 53*(2), 257–275.

Corpuz, E., Braybrook, A., Axleby, C., Trevitt, S., Campbell, E., Armstrong, D., Thomas, L., et al. (2022). *Double jeopardy: the economic and social costs of keeping women behind bars.*

Dioso-Villa, R. (2015). A repository of wrongful convictions in Australia: First steps toward estimating prevalence and causal contributing factors. *Flinders Law Journal, 17*(2), 163–202.

Dixon, D. (2006). "A window into the interviewing process?" The audio-visual recording of police interrogation in New South Wales, Australia. *Policing & Society, 16*(4), 323–348.

Duce, M. (2024). Plea bargaining and the risk of wrongful convictions: A comparative overview. In M. Langer, M. McConville, & L. Marsh (Eds.), *Research handbook on plea bargaining and criminal justice* (pp. 278-297).

Durnian, L. (2020). 'I did not say that I would just have to swear in court and it would be alright': Police verballing practices in Queensland courts, 1926–61. *Australian Historical Studies, 51*(3), 250–265.

Flynn, A. (2011). 'Fortunately we in Victoria are not in that UK situation': Australian and United Kingdom legal perspectives on plea bargaining reform. *Deakin Law Review, 16*(2), 361–404.

Flynn, A., & Freiberg, A. (2018). *Plea negotiations: Pragmatic justice in an imperfect world.* Springer.

Gross, S. R., & O'brien, B. (2008). Frequency and predictors of false conviction: Why we know so little, and new data on capital cases. *Journal of Empirical Legal Studies, 5*(4), 927–962.

Holt, G. A. (2024). Reducing the risk of false guilty pleas: How has the disability Royal Commission addressed this pathway to wrongful conviction for people with intellectual disabilities? *Research and Practice in Intellectual and Developmental Disabilities, 11*, 1–13.

Hussemann, J., & Siegel, J. (2018). Pleading guilty: Indigent defendant perceptions of the plea process. *Tennessee Journal of Law and Policy, 13*(2), 459–522.

Iftene, A., & Kinnear, V. L. (2020). Mr. Big and the new common law confessions rule: Five years in review. *Man. LJ, 43*, 295.

Jones, S. (2011). Under pressure: Women who plead guilty to crimes they have not committed. *Criminology & Criminal Justice, 11*(1), 77–90.

Lansdell, G. T., Saunders, B., Eriksson, A., & Bunn, R. (2021). What do lawyers really know about neurodisability? Confusion, obfuscation and dereliction of duty. In *Neurodisability and the Criminal Justice System* (pp. 153–175). Edward Elgar Publishing.

Mack, K., & Roach Anleu, S. (1995). Balancing principle and Pramatism: Guilty pleas. *Journal of Judicial Administration, 4*, 233–244.

Mansoor, H. S. (2020). Guilty until proven guilty: Effective bail reform as a human rights imperative. *DePaul Law Review, 70*, 15.

McConville, M., & Marsh, L. (2014). *Criminal judges: Legitimacy, courts and state-induced guilty pleas in Britain*. Edward Elgar Publishing.

McGregor, S. (2023). *Inquest into the passing of Veronica Nelson* (COR 2020 0021).

McMahon, M. (2019). *No bail, more jail?* Breaking the nexus between community protection and escalating pre-trial detention.

McQuire, A. (2019). White justice, black suffering: Extracting false confessions. *Griffith Review, 65*, 213–227.

Moffa, M., Freiberg, A., & Flynn, A. (2024). Women and victims: Neglected voices in plea negotiations. In M. Langer, M. McConville, & L. Marsh (Eds.), *Research handbook on plea bargaining and criminal justice* (pp. 392–408). Edward Elgar Publishing.

Nash, C., Dioso-Villa, R., & Porter, L. (2024). Factors contributing to guilty plea wrongful convictions: A quantitative analysis of Australian appellate court judgments. *Crime & Delinquency, 70*(2), 441–465.

National Registry of Exonerations. *Guilty Pleas.* Retrieved 07/11/2024 from https://www.law.umich.edu/special/exoneration/Pages/Guilty-Pleas.aspx

National Registry of Exonerations. (2015). *Guilty Pleas and False Confessions.* https://www.law.umich.edu/special/exoneration/Documents/NRE.Guilty.Plea.Article4.pdf

New South Wales Office of the Director of Public Prosecutions. (2023). *Annual Report 2022–2023.* Retrieved 07/11/2024 from https://www.odpp.nsw.gov.au/sites/default/files/2023-12/ODPP_Annual_Report_2022-2023_0.pdf

New South Wales Police Integrity Commission. (2004). *Report to parliament operation Florida*, volume 1. https://www.opengov.nsw.gov.au/publications/16617

Prosecutions, O. o. P. (2023). Office of Public Prosecutions Victoria Annual Report 2022/2023. O. o. P. Prosecutions. https://www.opp.vic.gov.au/wp-content/uploads/2024/02/OPP-Annual-Report-2022-23-final.pd

Redlich, A. D., Wilford, M. M., & Bushway, S. (2017). Understanding guilty pleas through the lens of social science. *Psychology, Public Policy, and Law, 23*(4), 458–472.

Roach, K. (2015). Comparative reflections on miscarriages of justice in Australia and Canada. *Flinders Law Journal, 17*(2), 381–431.

Roach, K. (2021). *You say you want a revolution?: Understanding guilty plea wrongful convictions.* Available at: https://ssrn.com/abstract=3869888.

Roach Anleu, S. L., & Mack, K. (2009). Intersections between in-court procedures and the production of guilty pleas. *Australian & New Zealand Journal of Criminology, 42*(1), 1–23.

Schehr, R., & French, C. (2015). Mental competency law and plea bargaining: A neurophenomenological critique. *Albany Law Review, 79*(3), 1091–1182.

Russell, E., Carlton, B., Tyson, D., Zhou, H., Pearce, M., & Faulkner, J. (2020). *A constellation of circumstances: The drivers of women's increasing rates of remand in Victoria.*

Ruyters, M., & Bartle, J. (2024). Who's watching Mr Big? Scenario operations and induced confessions. *Current Issues in Criminal Justice*, 1–16.

Stevenson, N. (1982). *Research report 9: A study of evidence presented to the district court in New South Wales.* D. o. t. A. G. o. J. N. B. o. C. S. Research. https://bocsar.nsw.gov.au/research-evaluations/1982/rr09-a-study-of-evidence-to-the-district-court-in-new-south-wales.html

Stratton, G., & Moffa, M. (2023). False allegations and wrongful convictions. In *Forensic psychology, crime and policing* (pp. 318–323). Policy Press.

van Buuren, J. (2024). Justice in English-only. *Social & Legal Studies, 33*(2), 191–212.

Wiseman, S. R. (2016). Fixing bail. *The George Washington Law Review, 84*, 417.

Wright, A. (2023). Bail Amendment Bill 2023. Parliamentary Library and Information Service. Retrieved from https://www.parliament.vic.gov.au/4a7d73/globalassets/images/news/library-papers/2023_5_bailamendmentbill-_rn_billbrief.pdf

Wood, J. (1997). Royal Commission into the New South Wales police service: Final report. In (Vol. 1): New South Wales Government Printer, .

CHAPTER 9

Capacity of Systems: The Management of Resources

Abstract This chapter examines how resource management impacts the capacity of the criminal justice system to address miscarriages of justice. Prompted by the significant challenges posed by inadequate legal aid funding, we highlight how this deficiency hinders defence lawyers' ability to conduct thorough investigations and prepare adequately, increasing the risk of wrongful convictions. The chapter also addresses the impact of the growing volume and complexity of evidence, especially digital data and covert recordings, which creates additional burdens to defence, prosecution, and law enforcement. Funding constraints exacerbate these issues, limiting the time available for crucial tasks like reviewing extensive materials and scrutinising police evidence, as illustrated by the case of a detective falsifying evidence. These pressures contribute to delays, stress, and potential procedural errors for both defence and prosecution.

Keyword Wrongful conviction • Legal aid • Funding • Digital data • Covert recordings • Resources

Inadequate legal assistance presents the most acute risk of wrongful conviction. This chapter considers the impact of insufficient funding, which limits the ability of defence lawyers to conduct thorough investigations, engage in independent investigations, or dedicate adequate time to case

M. Ruyters et al., *Innocence Unveiled*,
https://doi.org/10.1007/978-3-031-91343-3_9

preparation. The ongoing crisis of legal aid funding creates a systemic disadvantage, particularly in complex cases involving voluminous evidence, such as covert recordings or extensive digital data. Mounting caseloads, exacerbated by the complexities of modern trials and the backlog caused by the COVID-19 pandemic, have also strained prosecutorial resources. The cumulative impact of these pressures contributes to delays, stress, and potentially a higher likelihood of procedural errors, including non-disclosure breaches.

The chapter also examines the challenges posed by the sheer volume of evidence, particularly digital data and covert recordings. Advances in technology have revolutionised evidence collection but have also introduced significant burdens for defence, prosecution, and law enforcement. With cases involving vast amounts of telephone intercepts, text messages, and other digital files, the ability of the police and prosecution to effectively analyse, disclose, and present evidence is increasingly compromised.

Legal Resourcing

Inadequate legal aid funding is the most significant risk factor for wrongful convictions. Limited funding often limits defence lawyers to attempts to undermine the prosecution case rather than carrying out investigations that might result in independent evidence such as an alibi witness or the testing or re-testing of forensic evidence (Flynn et al., 2016, p. 228; Green, 2012, p. 48; Westminster Commission on Miscarriages of Justice, 2021, pp. 40–41). Funding constraints inevitably impact the time defence lawyers need to prepare cases for trial, including the time needed to read, watch, or listen to the case materials. The limited paid preparation time also increases the likelihood of defence lawyers failing to identify alternative defence strategies or overlooking material that was not disclosed by the prosecution and police.

An example of the need for the defence and prosecution to have adequate time to scrutinise the police case was illustrated in a recent case in Victoria, where a drug squad detective was convicted of falsifying evidence in a drug trafficking case. The detective forged DNA and handwriting analysis reports to falsely implicate the defendant in a drug house. The misconduct was only detected when the defence sought to cross-examine the forensic experts at the committal hearing. The handwriting expert identified the document concerned as a forgery (*DPP v Symes* [2024] VCC 1836; Pearson, 2024).

Modern trials are also increasingly more complex, involving voluminous materials, particularly cases involving many hours of covert recordings. Funding bodies impose significant constraints on preparation fees in most criminal cases. For example, Victoria Legal Aid (VLA) only permits counsel to claim fees for reviewing specific portions of video or audio recordings, leaving them with the choice of either reviewing the entire material without compensation or restricting their review to the content which can be digested within the limits of the funded period (Victoria Legal Aid, 2024). These challenges are particularly pronounced in complex trials, which can involve hundreds of hours of telephone intercepts and listening device recordings. The issue is further exacerbated when these recordings are of conversations in Languages Other than English (LOTE) and of poor quality, making accurate review even more difficult.

A 2008 review highlighted that fee constraints might lead VLA-funded barristers to take on multiple cases or proceed without adequate preparation (PricewaterhouseCoopers, 2008, p. 3). The Australian Law Council has warned in 2019 and 2023 that the legal assistance sector was 'under-resourced and under extreme pressure' (Law Council of Australia, 2023; Law Council of Australia, 2019, p. 7). A recent review of the National Legal Assistance Partnership (NLAP) also concluded that current funding for the legal assistance sector is insufficient to address rising cost pressures, growing demand for services, and increasingly complex legal needs (Mundy, 2024, p. 125). This finding is reflected in a legal aid funding crisis in the Northern Territory in 2024 which threatened to delay trials due to lack of legal representation (Dick, 2024).

More than half of Australian criminal cases receive legal aid funding (Richards & Trevallion, 2023). In the 2023–2024 financial year, 128, 590 applications for legal aid assistance with a criminal matter were made nationally (National Legal Aid, 2023–2024). Of those applications, 109,014 were approved and 12,157 were refused. However, in most of those cases, it is likely that funding is very limited. For instance, in Victoria over the 2022–2023 financial year, 41,239 applications were approved from a total of 44,001 applications received for all law types (Criminal, Civil, Family, and Unknown). The applications included 27, 891 applications for funding in criminal cases, of which 26,765 were approved (National Legal Aid, 2023–2024). Over the same period, case-related payments from Legal Aid to private solicitors, barristers, medical experts, interpreters, and third parties for all law types over the same period were $119.5 million (Victoria Legal Aid, 2023). The report did not include a separate breakdown for criminal cases. This works out to approximately $290 in funding for each approved application.

Prosecution bodies have also faced substantial backlogs due to COVID postponements, increasingly complex trials, high-profile cases, and delays in cases reaching trial (Garvey, 2024; Rintoul, 2024). For several years, prosecutors have described working long hours, heavy caseloads, inadequate funding, and stressful work environments (e.g. Easton, 2019; Houston & Mills, 2022). The workplace culture of the South Australian Office of the Director of Public Prosecutions was described as the "Hunger Games" and "untenable" in 2023 (Kelsall, 2023; Rix, 2023) while a 2024 New South Wales DPP staff survey revealed hundreds of staff experiencing unmanageable stress (Dudley, 2024) despite a ruling for a new award in 2023 intended to address an "unsustainable culture of overwork" (Dudley, 2023).

Voluminous Materials

The increasing complexity and volume of materials in criminal proceedings present an overwhelming difficulty for many defendants, particularly with digital data. Police and other investigative agencies use listening devices, telephone intercepts, and surveillance cameras to collect evidence in their investigations. The Commonwealth Director of Public Prosecutions ("CDPP") publishes complexity ratings for criminal cases which consider the size and volume of the evidence, the volume and complexity of forensic evidence, and the form in which the evidence is provided. Examples of a very difficult prosecution and extremely difficult prosecution (Complexity 3 and 4) include drug matters involving multi-agency investigations which include extensive use telephone intercept and surveillance device materials (CDPP, 2021).

Listening device recordings can be in place 24 hours a day over a period of weeks or even months, resulting in hundreds, if not thousands, of hours of recordings. In cases involving organised crime activity, it is not uncommon for numerous phones including 'burner' mobile phones to be "tapped" leading to thousands of text messages and phone calls. Telephone intercept warrants are obtained under *Telecommunications (Interception and Access) Act* 1979 (Cth). Warrants can also be obtained for access to stored communications data, namely, the content of communication data that was transmitted by a telecommunication network and is being stored by the network. Over the period 2022–2023, 3210 interception warrants and 795 stored communication warrants were issued to Australian authorised interception agencies, 334,237 authorisations for disclosure of existing telecommunications data, primarily for serious drug offences (Attorney-General's Department, 2023, p. viii). The volume of electronic material collected during investigations is also increasing, with even a single mobile phone typically containing a 'vast quantity of data' (CDPP, 2019, p. 9).

The ubiquity of mobile telephone data puts pressure on the defence to be pro-active in seeking data extracted from a defendant's mobile phone. In *Edwards v The Queen* [2021] HCA 28, the High Court had different views on whether mandatory pre-trial disclosure requirements in the *Criminal Procedure Act 1986* (NSW) required a large amount of phone data to be disclosed. The police had downloaded over 60,000 files, including over 20,000 text messages, from Edward's seized mobile telephone (*Edwards,* 2021, [1]), Kiefel CJ, Keane and Gleeson JJ). The prosecution disclosed the existence of the download but did not provide the downloaded materials prior to trial. It was not until the end of the trial that the defence requested a copy of the download, which was eventually provided after Edward was convicted. The Court was unanimous in rejecting the appeal as the failure to disclose the electronic evidence did not give rise to a miscarriage of justice. While there were different approaches to the scope of the disclosure duty, the court held that the defence, even after accessing the data, was unable to identify how the contents would assist the defence ([25], Kiefel CJ, Keana and Gleeson JJ; [35], Edelman and Steward JJ).

The vast volume of digital data collected by investigators has become a considerable burden for police, prosecution, and defence (Collie, 2018; Wilson-Kovacs et al., 2023). In a 2023 UK study of criminal defence lawyers, respondents reported dealing with an unmanageable and overwhelming volume of evidence, commenting:

> 1 GB of data is about 900,000 pages of text messages, 300 photos, 120,000 documents…when you] have between 64 GB to 2 TB of data, it takes a long time to work through the data. (S34) (Wilson-Kovacs et al., 2023, p. 243)

High-volume-evidence cases also make it difficult for police and prosecution to comply with their disclosure duties, leading to disclosable material not being adequately assessed for relevance and remaining undisclosed (RCMPI, 2020, pp. 33–34). It is also common for police to paste selected evidence retrieved from digital data and telephone call logs into spreadsheets, which are disclosed alongside digital files. As these records indicate, the evidence that the prosecution will rely on at trial, defence lawyers with minimal time for preparation are more likely to rely on that curated information than conduct their own investigations of the digital data (Wilson-Kovacs et al., 2023, pp. 243–244).

The complexity of the challenges posed by high-volume digital evidence is compounded when dealing with covert recordings, particularly those involving indistinct audio or conversations in languages other than English.

Covert Recordings

Complex trials can involve hundreds, if not thousands, of hours of covert recordings obtained from telephone intercepts and listening devices in languages other than English, and which are often of a very poor and indistinct quality. Covert conversations about illegal activity also often involve the use of code words. One of the problems is that these kinds of recordings are also usually translated directly into English rather than being first transcribed in the original language, as is the case in the US (Gilbert & Heydon, 2021). The voices on those recordings also need to be identified or attributed to different speakers by people who do not necessarily have expertise or familiarity with the voices. These issues increase significantly in complex trials that involve hundreds of courses of covert recordings, particularly when the conversations on the recordings are in languages other than English (LOTE) and when the recordings are of poor quality.

In Australia, LOTE recordings are also usually translated directly into English rather than being first transcribed in the original language, as is the case in the US (Gilbert & Heydon, 2021, p. 2), which can impact the accuracy of the translation. The voices on those recordings are identified or attributed to different speakers by people who do not necessarily have expertise or familiarity with the voices (French & Fraser, 2018), adding to the matters that should be checked by counsel—if there was funded time to do so. Helen Fraser has also written extensively about the dangers of priming judges and juries with transcripts of recordings, which have been provided to assist their perception of poor-quality recordings (Fraser, 2021; Fraser & Kinoshita, 2021; Fraser & Stevenson, 2014). This will particularly be an issue where police have recorded and prepared the transcripts because of the inherent case bias they might bring to interpreting indistinct words and phrases.

Legislation

Criminal Procedure Act 1986 (NSW)
Telecommunications (Interception and Access) Act 1979 (Cth)

Cases

Edwards v The Queen [2021] HCA 28
DPP v Symes [2024] VCC 1836

References

Attorney-General's Department. (2023). *2022–2023 Annual Report under the Telecommunications (interception and Access) Act 1979 and Part 15 of the Telecommunications Act 1997*. A.-G. s. Department. https://www.ag.gov.au/sites/default/files/2024-03/tia-act-annual-report-2022-23.PDF

Collie, J. (2018). Digital forensic evidence-flaws in the criminal justice system. *Forensic Science International, 289*, 154–155.

Commonwealth Director of Public Prosecutions ("CDPP"). (2021). National Legal Directions: Complexity ratings December 2021. In.

Commonwealth Director of Public Prosecutions ("DCPP"). (2019). Royal Commission into the Management of Police Informants, submission by the commonwealth director of public prosecutions -disclosure issues December 2019. In.

Dick, S. (2024). *Funding crisis at legal aid NT threatens to undermine territory's justice system*. https://www.abc.net.au/news/2024-10-30/legal-aid-nt-funding-crisis-begins-influencing-supreme-court/104532140

Dudley, E. (2023, 29/10/2023). More benefits for 'overworked prosecutors': Ruling. *The Australian*. https://www.theaustralian.com.au/nation/more-benefits-for-overworked-prosecutors-ruling/news-story/562ba60ef3a5e73a137563ff9640818d?amp&nk=53d764114c69dd518421d6a3476c6343-1698712922

Dudley, E. (2024). 'Burnout, unmanageable stress': NSW DPP staff survey results revealed. *The Weekend Australian*. https://www.theaustralian.com.au/nation/burnout-unmanageable-stress-nsw-dpp-staff-survey-results-revealed/news-story/e12bdbc7ed10b3ea3722694abaad7a55

Easton, S. (2019, 26/11/2019). *CPSU: ACT public prosecutors overworked, underpaid and hungry for flexible work*. https://www.themandarin.com.au/121309-cpsu-act-public-prosecutors-overworked-underpaid-and-hungry-for-flexible-work/

Flynn, A., Hodgson, J., McCulloch, J., & Naylor, B. (2016). Legal aid and access to legal representation: Redefining the right to a fair trial. *The Melbourne University Law Review, 40*, 207.

Fraser, H. (2021). Enhancing and priming at a voir dire: Can we be sure the judge reached the right conclusion? *Australian Journal of Forensic Sciences, 53*(2), 224–251.

Fraser, H., & Kinoshita, Y. (2021). Injustice arising from the unnoticed power of priming: How lawyers and even judges can be misled by unreliable transcripts of indistinct forensic audio. *Criminal Law Journal, 45*(3), 142–152.

Fraser, H., & Stevenson, B. (2014). The power and persistence of contextual priming: More risks in using police transcripts to aid jurors' perception of poor quality covert recordings. *The International Journal of Evidence & Proof, 18*(3), 205–229.

French, P., & Fraser, H. (2018). Why "ad hoc experts" should not provide transcripts of indistinct audio, and a better approach. *Criminal Law Journal*, 298–302.

Garvey, P. (2024, 03/11/2024). WA legal system groaning as shortages of silk, courtooms bite. *The Australian Business Review*. https://www.theaustralian.com.au/business/legal-affairs/wa-legal-system-groaning-as-shortages-of-silk-courtrooms-bite/news-story/10bc8a40c9a2b960153f7573ab05cde8

Gilbert, D., & Heydon, G. (2021). Translated transcripts from covert recordings used for evidence in court: Issues of reliability. *Frontiers in Communication, 6*, 779227.

Green, A. (2012). Challenging the refusal to investigate evidence neglected by trial lawyers. In *The criminal cases review commission* (pp. 46–58). Springer.

Houston, C., & Mills, T. (2022, 01/05/2022). 'Toxic' OPP in turmoil, with solicitor exodus after sex offence unit axed. *The Age*. https://www.theage.com.au/politics/victoria/toxic-opp-in-turmoil-with-solicitor-exodus-after-sex-offence-unit-axed-20220429-p5ah2z.html

Kelsall, T. (2023, 29/08/2023). *Report finds DPP workplace experience 'untenable', calls for broader review*. https://www.indaily.com.au/news/2023/08/29/report-finds-dpp-workplace-experience-untenable-calls-for-broader-reviewLaw Council of Australia. (2019). *2019–20 Pre-Budget Submission*. Retrieved 21/10/2024 from https://lawcouncil.au/publicassets/b8630bd9-6440-e911-93fc-005056be13b5/3578%20-%20Pre-Budget%20Submission%202019.pdf

Law Council of Australia. (2023). *Funding for legal assistance services more urgent in tough time*. Retrieved 21/10/2024 from https://lawcouncil.au/media/media-releases/funding-for-legal-assistance-services-more-urgent-in-tough-times

Mundy, W. (2024). *Independent Review of the National Legal Assistance Partnership.* https://www.ag.gov.au/sites/default/files/2024-06/NLAP-review-report.PDF

National Legal Aid. (2023–2024). *National Legal Aid Statistics.* Retrieved 20/10/2024 from nla.legalaid.nsw.gov.au/NLAReports/reportviewer.aspx?reportname=ApplicationStatus

Pearson, E. (2024). *Jail for drug squad cop for falsifying DNA evidence in trafficking case.* https://www.theage.com.au/national/victoria/jail-for-drug-squad-cop-for-falsifying-dna-evidence-in-trafficking-case-20241119-p5krpa.html

PricewaterhouseCoopers. (2008). *Victorian Bar: Review of fees paid by Victoria legal aid to barristers in criminal cases.*

Richards, S., & Trevallion, J. (2023). The impact of stagnant legal aid rates on access to justice in Australia. *Jurist.*

Rintoul, C. (2024). State budget 2024: Overworked state prosecution office to get $3.1 million boost and new team to tackle backlog. *The West Australian.* https://thewest.com.au/news/court-justice/state-budget-2024-overworked-state-prosecution-office-to-get-31m-boost-and-new-team-to-tackle-case-backlog-c-14374515

Rix, E. (2023, 30/08/2023). SA prosecutors' office likened to hunger games in damning review of workplace culture. *ABC News.* https://www.abc.net.au/news/2023-08-30/office-of-sa-dpp-compared-to-hunger-games/102793414

Royal Commission into the Management of Police Informants. (2020). *Final report*, volume 4, November 2020. V. G. Printer.

Victoria Legal Aid. Victoria Legal Aid Additional Preparation Worksheet Counsel Jan 2024 Fees. Retrieved 21/10/24 from https://www.handbook.vla.vic.gov.au/node/5731

Victoria Legal Aid. (2023). *Annual report 2022–23 access to justice for Victorians.* https://content.legalaid.vic.gov.au/sites/default/files/2023-11/vla-annual-report-2022-2023.pdf

Westminster Commission on Miscarriages of Justice. (2021). *In the interest of justice: An inquiry into the criminal cases review commission.* https://appgmiscarriagesofjustice.wordpress.com/commission-on-miscarriages-of-justice/

Wilson-Kovacs, D., Helm, R., Growns, B., & Redfern, L. (2023). Digital evidence in defence practice: Prevalence, challenges and expertise. *The International Journal of Evidence & Proof, 27*(3), 235–253.

CHAPTER 10

Managerialism: The Cost of Efficiency

Abstract This chapter highlights how the pursuit of efficiency and cost-effectiveness through managerialism has significantly shaped the Australian criminal justice system. We argue that managerialist policies expedite procedures, potentially undermining the fundamental principles of due process and introducing systemic vulnerabilities. From flawed forensic practices and disproportionate over-policing targeting Indigenous communities to almost insurmountable barriers in appellate processes, a focus on outcomes amplifies the risk of wrongful convictions. The pressure for quick resolutions fosters plea bargaining, even for the innocent, and resource constraints within legal aid further disadvantage vulnerable individuals. In courts, restrictive appeal mechanisms, driven by managerialist objectives, impede the rectification of errors. While the mode of trial presents a complex dynamic, the overarching impact of managerialism necessitates a critical examination of its cost to justice.

Keyword Wrongful conviction • Managerialism • Efficiency • Due process • Cost-effectiveness • Appeals

Like many other Western democracies, the Australian criminal justice system has emphasised managerialism that prioritises efficiency and cost-effectiveness. Managerialism often results in policies that expedite criminal

M. Ruyters et al., *Innocence Unveiled*,
https://doi.org/10.1007/978-3-031-91343-3_10

justice procedures, potentially undermining due process. An emphasis on resource management introduces systemic vulnerabilities to error from flawed forensic processes to over-policing strategies disproportionately targeting Indigenous communities. Managerialist approaches in the courts also create almost insurmountable obstacles to remedying wrongful convictions. As this chapter explores, managerialist policies in policing, forensic science, and courts show how outcomes focus increases the risk of wrongful convictions, particularly amongst the most vulnerable in the community.

Vulnerability to Error

These process risks expose Indigenous people to an increased risk of wrongful conviction, leading to over-policing and a higher likelihood of arrest and charges (MacFarlane & Stratton, 2016). This emphasis on efficiency can also create a reluctance to acknowledge and investigate potential wrongful convictions, as they might be viewed as occurring at a 'manageable' rate. For instance, NSW Police introduced a Suspect Target Management Plan (STMP), a preventative policing policy that involves 'targets' being consistently monitored and observed (LECC, 2023, p. 6). The policy had a disproportionate impact on Indigenous children, with more than 70% of young people on the STMP identified as Aboriginal (LECC, 2023, p. 36). Flaunted as 'proactive policing', STMP relied heavily on flawed algorithms to target young people to interrupt criminal behaviour by 'proactively engaging high-risk and prolific suspects' (LECC, 2023, p. 6). The monitoring and deterrent aims of the STMP policy raise significant challenges to the presumption of innocence and right to liberty, mainly when errors occur in the database all in the names of cost-effectiveness and resource allocation (Englezos, 2023).

Managerialist objectives also include risk quality assurance. For instance, the 2022 Commission of Inquiry ("Sofronoff Inquiry") into forensic DNA testing at Queensland Health Forensic and Scientific Services (QHFSS) discussed in Chap. 4, highlighted significant failures within the laboratory, primarily stemming from a managerial focus on speed over accuracy in DNA testing. A second inquiry into the same laboratory noted that the "understandable desire" for 'efficiency and to overcome a backlog of important samples for testing seems to have superseded the need for scientific accountability and scientific integrity" (Bennett, 2023, p. 3).

More than 40,000 cases were subject to review and have led to new appeals (Burt, 2024; Siganto, 2024).

Similarly, the priorities of managerialist policies frequently lead to the underfunding of public prosecutions and legal aid services, creating a significant disadvantage for anyone navigating the complexity of the legal system. Lawyers working with legal aid worldwide face resource constraints, often compelling them to prioritise severe cases, leaving those charged with less serious offences without adequate representation and vulnerable to error. This lack of adequate legal representation can result in a failure to identify and challenge errors in the criminal justice process, further increasing the risk of wrongful conviction.

The pressure to resolve cases quickly, driven by managerialism and political pressure, can also lead to plea bargaining suggestions, where individuals, including potentially innocent ones, may feel compelled to plead guilty to avoid lengthy and costly trials. Plea negotiations are structured into a case conferencing system which is managed by the courts (Flynn & Freiberg, 2018, p. 90). As we discussed earlier, his pressure is particularly concerning for Indigenous peoples who are already over-represented in the criminal justice system and may be more vulnerable to coercion or tactics aimed at securing a conviction. MacFarlane and Stratton (2016) recognised the cases of Robyn Kina (*R v Kina* [1993] QCA 480), Basil Dumoo (*Dumoo v Donald Anthony Garner* (1997) 7 NTLR 129), and Ian, Gary, and Vivian Campbell, and Brett and Steven Rotumah (*Campbell v Director of Public Prosecutions* (2008) NSWSC 1284) as potential wrongful convictions where managerialist approaches exacerbated miscarriages of justice.

Managerialist policies in Australian courts not only increase the risk of wrongful convictions but represent the most significant barrier to addressing them. These policies are particularly evident in the appellate gatekeeping role, where rules such as requiring leave for appeals beyond those involving questions of law restrict the number of cases progressing to appeal. In 2021–22, appeals represented only 0.012% of finalised criminal cases (Productivity Commission, 2023). These measures are aimed to prevent unmeritorious claims from overwhelming courts but potentially exclude many cases of factual innocence that cannot meet narrow appeal criteria, such as fresh evidence requirements (Ruyters & Bartle, 2024).

A threshold of fresh evidence for many post-conviction claims is a critical constraint on cases progressing to appeal. This is because fresh evidence must be evidence that was not reasonably available to the accused during the trial. If the defence failed to call evidence they reasonably should have been aware of at trial, that evidence cannot be considered 'fresh' and an appeal court is unlikely to find a miscarriage of justice (*Ratten v The Queen* (1974) 131 CLR 510, 517). Fresh evidence is especially critical for second and subsequent appeal rights which were first introduced in South Australia in 2013 and are also available in Tasmania, Victoria, Western Australia, Queensland, and the Australian Capital Territory. In line with their managerialist objectives, these subsequent appeal rights are very narrow with all requiring evidence to be both 'fresh' and 'compelling.' By 2024, there were only five successful second and further appeals across all six jurisdictions (Ruyters & Bartle, 2024, p. 4). The emphasis on freshness assumes that defendants are aware of evidence that might be used in their defence. As discussed earlier, defendants may be unaware of the impact of their lawyers' strategic decisions or may have difficulty understanding all their case materials (Ruyters & Bartle, 2024, p. 4). There may, however, be some benefits for defendants in managerialist approaches.

Jury or Judge-Alone Trials

Some research indicates that judge-alone trials result in higher acquittal rates than jury trials, but the evidence is inconsistent and may reflect that judge-alone trials are heard far less frequently than jury trials (Gu, 2024; Sager et al., 2022). For example, in 1993, the acquittal rate in judge-alone trials in the New South Wales District and Supreme Courts was 62.4% compared to the 52.3% acquittal rate for jury trials, although it should be noted that the judge-alone trials represented only 7% of the total trials in the period. The difference in outcome increased in 1999, with 67.3% of judge-alone and 48.2% of jury trials resulting in acquittals. Similar patterns were recorded in 2005 and 2007, although judge-alone trials only accounted for 29 of 629 trials in 2005 and 35 of 497 trials in 2007 (Krisenthal, 2016, p. 18). From 2009, however, jury trials resulted in higher acquittal rates than judge-alone trials (Krisenthal, 2016, p. 19).

Gu's larger 2024 study analysed 5064 jury trials and 805 judge-alone trials in 2011–2019, examining the probability of acquittal, court efficiency outcomes, and sentencing severity. Gu found that judge-alone trials were linked to a 12-percentage point higher likelihood of acquittal compared to jury trials, even when controlled for factors influencing trial outcomes (Gu, 2024, p. 31). One of the reasons offered for higher judge-alone acquittal rates is that judges are required to provide reasons for their decisions to justify the verdict (Gu, 2024, pp. 9, 22; s. 133(2) *Criminal Procedure Act 1986* (NSW); Krisenthal, 2016, p. 19). Jury's decision-making in Australia is secret on the other hand, and juries are prohibited from publishing statements, opinions, and arguments made during their deliberations (see e.g. *Juries Act 2000* (Vic) s 78). Judge-alone trials were also perceived as more efficient as they were shorter, relying more on written submissions, and shorter presentations of evidence (Gu, 2024, p. 31; Percy & Barnes, 2020, p. 22), although it is unclear how realistic this is in the context of a criminal trial. Judge-alone trials are shorter because there is no need to empanel juries, provide directions, and no need for time for deliberation. Judge-alone trials are also more cost-effective as the costs of court security and staffing and payments to jurors are reduced (Percy & Barnes, 2020, p. 22).

Criticisms of jury trials often centre on the potential for bias (Ruva & Coy, 2020; *R v Cant* [2002] NTCCA 8). Jurors can be influenced by inadmissible evidence through social media and internet searching or making other inquiries about the case. Potential misuse of information has included commenting or publishing information about the case (McNeill, 2016; *Agelakis v The Queen* [2020] NSWCCA 72; *Attorney General for Western Australia v Marijanich* [2024] WASC 312), researching the case (Knaus, 2022; Whitbourn, 2024; *R v K* (2003) NSWCCA 406; *R v Folbigg* [2007] NSWCCA 371), contacting parties or witnesses and lawyers (e.g., Deans, 2011), or seeking other people's opinions about the case (Weber, 2024). There are also fears that jurors can also be overwhelmed by skilled lawyers, complex legal principles, and complex facts (Croucher & Hon, 2022, p. 85).

Other concerns are the influence of pretrial publicity about high-profile defendants (Hews, 2019; McEwen et al., 2018). For instance, Lloyd Rayney was a high-profile Crown prosecutor charged with murdering his estranged wife, Corryn Rayney in August 2007. Corryn was also well known as a registrar of the Supreme Court. The case attracted extensive pretrial publicity. The police identified Rayney as a person of interest during extensive media coverage of Corryn's funeral, and one detective subsequently identified Rayney as the prime and only suspect in the murder investigation at a media conference in September 2007 (*The State of Western Australia v Rayney* [2011] WASC 326, [49, [54], [93]). Commissioner Sleight granted the trial by judge-alone. The Commissioner found that the police announcement of Rayney as the main suspect increased interest in the case, and the long period of time between the announcement and Rayney subsequently being charged meant 'that the prejudice created against Mr Rayney is likely to have become well entrenched' (*Rayney,* 2011, [88]). Rayney was subsequently acquitted (*The State of Western Australia v Rayney* [No 3] [2012] WASC 404). A prosecution appeal against the judgment of acquittal was unsuccessful (*The State of Western Australia v Rayney* [2013] WASCA 219). There were similar concerns about the extent and duration of pretrial publicity in the case of Stefan Schmidt. Schmidt had been convicted of murder by a jury in 2012 for pushing a musician out a hotel window. At a retrial following a successful appeal, he was granted a judge-alone trial because of pretrial publicity around his first trial, the verdict, and his appeal (*Schmidt v The State of Western Australia [No 3]* [2014] WASC 156 [41]).

Judge-alone trials are only available to defendants in the Australian Capital Territory New South Wales, Western Australia, and Queensland, although Victoria briefly introduced judge-alone trials when jury trials were suspended during the COVID-19 pandemic. As an example, the defendant and prosecution can both apply for a judge-alone trial in New South Wales under the s132 *Criminal Procedure Act 1986* (NSW). The defendant must agree with the prosecution's application and the court may order a trial by judge if the prosecution do not agree with the defendant's application for a judge-alone trial if it considers it is in the interests of justice to do so (*Criminal Procedure Act 1986* (NSW) s 132(3), (4)). The issue of "judge shopping," however, has been raised numerous times in the context of judge-alone trials (*R v Perry* (193) 29 NSWLR 589, p. 594, Gleeson CJ; *Alameddine v The King* [2022 NSWCCA 219; *R v Simmons No 4* [2015] NSWSC 259), although s132A(1) *Criminal Procedure Act 1986* (NSW) section 132A(1) provides some protection against this.

The mode of trial is a potential risk for wrongful convictions but may also be a roll of the dice for defendants.

Legislation

Criminal Procedure Act 1986 (NSW).
Juries Act 2000 (Vic)

Cases

Agelakis v The Queen [2020] NSWCCA 72
Alameddine v The King [2022 NSWCCA 219
Attorney General for Western Australia v Marijanich [2024] WASC 312
Campbell v Director of Public Prosecutions (2008) NSWSC 1284
Dumoo v Donald Anthony Garner (1997) 7 NTLR 129
R v Birks (1990) 19 NSWLR 677
R v Cant [2002] NTCCA 8
R v Folbigg [2007] NSWCCA 371
R v K (2003) NSWCCA 406
R v Kina [1993] QCA 480
R v Perry (193) 29 NSWLR 589
Ratten v The Queen (1974) 131 CLR 510
Schmidt v The State of Western Australia [No 3] [2014] WASC 156
Slater v The Queen [2020] VSCA 270]
The State of Western Australia v Rayney [2011] WASC 326
The State of Western Australia v Rayney [2013] WASCA 219

References

Bennett, A. (2023). *Final Report: Commission of inquiry to examine DNA project 13 concerns.* Queensland Government. https://www.dnaproject13inquiry.qld.gov.au/assets/DNA%20Project%2013%20Report.pdf

Burt, J. (2024). Queensland's forensics lab has reviewed less than two per cent of cases since inquiry. *ABC News.* https://www.abc.net.au/news/2024-04-20/queensland-dna-lab-review-forensics-inquiry-crime/103748990

Croucher, J. S., & Hon, S. (2022). Judge or jury? A legal conundrum. *International Journal of Criminal Justice Sciences, 17*(1), 83–92.

Deans, J. (2011). Facebook juror jailed for eight months. *The Guardian.* https://www.theguardian.com/uk/2011/jun/16/facebook-juror-jailed-for-eight-months

Englezos, E. (2023). Policing by algorithm: NSW Police's suspect target management plan. *Alternative Law Journal, 48*(1), 17–24.

Flynn, A., & Freiberg, A. (2018). *Report to the criminology research advisory council Grant: CRG 51/13-14.* https://www.aic.gov.au/sites/default/files/2020-05/CRG_51_13-14-FinalReport.pdf

Gu, J. (2024). *The effect of judge-alone trials on criminal justice outcomes* (Crime and justice bulletin, Issue. N. B. o. C. S. a. Research). https://bocsar.nsw.gov.au/documents/publications/cjb/cjb251-300/CJB264-Report-Effect-of-judge-alone-trials.pdf

Hews, R. J. (2019). *Twitter trials and Facebook juries: An analysis of the Australian sub judice rule and the regulation of prejudicial publicity on social media during high-profile criminal trials* Queensland University of Technology].

Knaus, C. (2022). Bruce Lehrmann trial aborted with jury discharged after outside material brought into jury room. *The Guardian*. https://www.theguardian.com/australia-news/2022/oct/27/jury-discharged-in-bruce-lehrmann-case-after-material-entered-jury-room-that-ought-not-to-have

Krisenthal, P. (2016). Judge alone trials in NSW: Practical considerations. In: *Criminal CPD*.

Law Enforcement Conduct Commission "LECC". (2023). *Operation Tepito—an investigation into the application of the NSW*.

MacFarlane, J., & Stratton, G. (2016). Marginalisation, managerialism and wrongful conviction in Australia. *Current Issues in Criminal Justice, 27*(3), 303–321.

McEwen, R., Eldridge, J., & Caruso, D. (2018). Differential or deferential to media? The effect of prejudicial publicity on judge or jury. *The International Journal of Evidence & Proof, 22*(2), 124–143.

McNeill, H. (2016). Calls to overhaul WA jury system after juror dismissed for Facebook post. *WA Today*. https://www.watoday.com.au/national/western-australia/calls-to-overhaul-wa-jury-system-after-juror-dismissed-for-facebook-post-20161012-gs0wwa.html

Percy, T., & Barnes, G. (2020). Trial by judge alone. *Precedent*(161).

Productivity Commission. (2023). *Report on Government Services 2023: Table 7A 1, pt C s 7* https://www.pc.gov.au/ongoing/report-on-government-services/2023/justice/courts

Ruva, C. L., & Coy, A. E. (2020). Your bias is rubbing off on me: The impact of pretrial publicity and jury type on guilt decisions, trial evidence interpretation, and impression formation. *Psychology, Public Policy, and Law, 26*(1), 22.

Ruyters, M., & Bartle, J. (2024). The problem of post-conviction review in Australia. *Alternative Law Journal*, 1037969X241289556.

Sager, B. R., Stinson, P. M., & Wentzlof, C. A. (2022). *Bench vs. Jury trials convictions and sentencing outcomes for arrested officers, 2005–2016*.

Siganto, T. (2024). Andrew John Cobby seeks appeal for murder conviction of wife Kym Cobby over Queensland DNA lab bungle. *ABC News*. https://www.abc.net.au/news/2024-06-04/andrew-cobby-seeks-appeal-murder-conviction-gold-coast-dna-lab/103933994

Sofronoff, W. (2022). *Final report: Commission of Inquiry into forensic DNA testing in Queensland*. https://www.health.qld.gov.au/__data/assets/pdf_file/0036/1196685/final-report-coi-dna-testing-qld-dec-2022.pdf

Weber, D. (2024). Rape trial juror Darren Marijanich found in contempt of WA court, ordered to pay almost $15,000. *ABC News*. https://www.abc.net.au/news/2024-09-02/juror-in-wa-rape-trial-fined-for-contempt-of-court/104301424

Whitbourn, M. (2024). How a dictionary derailed a Sydney criminal trial. *The Sydney Morning Herald*. https://www.smh.com.au/national/nsw/how-a-dictionary-derailed-a-sydney-criminal-trial-20241029-p5kmcd.html

CHAPTER 11

Balancing Secrecy and Transparency

Abstract This chapter examines how the balance between effective investigative techniques and the protection of individual rights can, when exploited, lead to wrongful convictions. We highlight the ethical and legal complexities surrounding covert methods, the use of informants, and credibility assessment tools deemed "junk science" such as SCAN and polygraphs. The chapter exposes the significant risk of wrongful convictions associated with unreliable informant evidence, particularly from incentivised testimony. The controversial 'Mr Big' scenario technique has raised significant concerns surrounding its potential for false confessions and the lack of independent oversight, raising concerns about its impact on justice.

Keywords Wrongful conviction • Investigative techniques • Informant • SCAN • Mr. Big

There is an often-tenuous balance between the need for effective investigative techniques and the protection of individual rights. This tension is particularly evidence in the use of covert methods, informants, and investigative tools that the courts regard as junk science, which involve ethical and legal complexities. While these techniques can be crucial in securing convictions or breakthroughs in cases, their misuse can lead to wrongful

M. Ruyters et al., *Innocence Unveiled*,
https://doi.org/10.1007/978-3-031-91343-3_11

convictions, and the lack of independent scrutiny over their use is a significant risk. This chapter explores key investigative methods, including the use of informants, covert operations such as the Mr. Big scenario operations, and the use of scientific content analysis and polygraphs as credibility assessment tools.

Deals with Witnesses (Immunities, Indemnities, and Undertakings)

Research from the United States has shown that false informer evidence is a significant factor in wrongful convictions (Garrett, 2011, 2015; Gould et al., 2013). Garrett reported in 2015 that 24% of the 330 DNA exonerations recorded at the time involved evidence from informants, including prison informants (Garrett, 2015, p. 12). While these categories overlap, we differentiate between immunities and indemnities offered to witnesses who may have been involved with the crime in question and agreements made with prison informants. For instance, the NSW prosecution guidelines define informer witnesses as any person who can provide information relevant to the matter and is either a co-offender or a person seeking to benefit from providing the information (ODPP, 2021, [11.3]). Prison informants, on the other hand, are generally not involved with the crime in question and are generally used to provide evidence of confessional statements made by the defendant while in prison (ODPP, 2021[11.3]; *Pollitt v The Queen* (1992) 174 CLR 558, p. 605, Toohey J). The use of prison informers is considered in the next section.

Typically, police have relied on public interest immunity claims to protect informers, including those who are not witnesses (*Royal Women's Hospital v Medical Practitioners Board* (2006) 15 VR 22, p. 46 per Charles JA; J *Jarvie v Magistrates' Court of Victoria at Brunswick* [1995] 1 VR 84; *Marks v Beyfus* (1890) LR 25 QBD 494). Public interest immunity protects the disclosure of classified and security-sensitive information in court proceedings and will typically prevent disclosure of the existence of the police informer to the defendant. Public interest immunity ("PII") claims require balancing competing public interests (see also *Uniform Evidence Acts* ("UEA") s130(1)), as the right of an accused to face their accusers is a fundamental human right—an essential component of a fair trial—and there is a public interest in disclosure (*Kant v DPP* (1994) 73 A Crim R 481, p. 493 per Kirby P; Lusty, 2002).

As with difficulties in challenging prison informants, the non-disclosure of a witness's identity restricts the accused's right to cross-examine the informer, including on whether they received benefits in return for their evidence, which may undermine their right to a fair trial. Consequently, the balance may tip towards disclosing the identity of the informer if that information is essential to establishing a person's innocence (*Carter v The Managing Partner, Northmore Hale Davy and Leake and Others* (1995) 183 CLR 121, Toohey J in dissent; *Alister v The Queen* (1984) 154 CLR 404, 456, Brennan J). If the risk to the informant is too great, the prosecution has the option of discontinuing the prosecution or seeking a stay of the proceedings. The withholding of information through PII claims, which are often heard *ex parte*, can, however, devastate a defendant's right to a fair trial, as this may mean the loss of access to potentially exculpatory information or identifying any abuse in the process.

The use of informers is considered crucial for police investigations, but it is also vulnerable to police corruption (OPI, Integrity, 2007a, 2007b, p. 10; McMurdo, 2020). The ethical and legal risks of human source management were starkly illustrated in the state of Victoria, where numerous prosecutions were potentially compromised when police used a criminal defence lawyer as an informant. Barrister Nicola Gobbo, known as 'Lawyer X', secretly acted as a police informant between 1995 to 2009 while representing high-profile gangland identities. Her covert role was revealed in March 2019 after the Court of Appeal and High Court found that the public interest in protecting Gobbo's identity as an informer was outweighed by the public interest in disclosure (*AB v CD & EF* [2017] VSCA 338; *AB v CD; EF v CD* [2018] HCA 58). The ensuing scandal prompted the establishment of the Royal Commission into the Management of Police Informants, which ultimately condemned Victoria Police's handling of human sources and recommended significant reforms to prevent similar ethical breaches in the future (McMurdo, 2020). Gobbo's informer role has led to the overturning of two convictions at the time of publication and others are likely (*Orman v The Queen* [2019] VSCA 163,[12]; See also *Cvetanovski v The Queen* [2020] VSCA 272).

The 'Golden Rule'

While Victoria Police have required the registration of informers since 1992 (Victoria Police Force Circular Memo, 1991), there was no risk assessment process until 2003, and the focus of processes introduced to manage human sources was primarily on maintaining confidentiality about the identity and location of informers for their safety (McMurdo, 2020, p. 211). This 'golden rule' is longstanding (Mares, 2002; McMurdo, 2020, pp. 211, 538) and reflected in the duty of care assumed by Victoria Police for Gobbo's ongoing safety and welfare and concerns about her transitioning from an informer to a witness in proceedings against a former Victorian Police Officer (McMurdo, 2020, pp. 194, 198).

The *Human Source Management Act* 2023 (Vic), which emerged from the Royal Commission, will provide for the registration, use, and management of human sources by Victoria Police and the external oversight of the use of human sources (s 1).[1] However, the legislation still prioritises the safety and confidentiality of police informants, and offences under Part 6 include intentionally or recklessly disclosing information likely to identity a source (s 87). Excepted 'permitted disclosures' defined in section 3 include '(b) disclosure for the purposes of any legal proceeding'.

Australian Directors of Public Prosecutions have guidelines on the disclosure of informer identities. For example, the NSW Prosecution Guidelines provide that where an informer is to be called as a witness, the prosecutor should, subject to 'legal professional privilege and PII, disclose all matters that would assist in evaluating the informer's evidence', including any motivation for giving evidence and benefits such as favourable treatment or reports, sentence discounts, monetary benefits, or grant of immunity (ODPPNSW, 2021, p. 41). Following the Royal Commission into the Management of Police Informants, the Victorian Office of Public Prosecutions has a separate protocol for resolving complex issues related to disclosure and PII claims. Where it is determined that the material should be the subject of a PII claim, the Victorian Government Solicitor's Office will seek court ruling (Office of Public Prosecutions, Victoria, 2022). As with s15A *Director of Public Prosecutions Act 1986* (NSW), however, the police will make the initial determination whether material will be subject to a PII claim, and it is unclear how this will prevent the non-disclosure practices of Victoria Police.

[1] The act was not yet in operation at the time of writing.

Informer Benefits: Indemnity from Prosecution and Undertaking as to Use of Evidence

The prosecution disclosure obligations include disclosing material that is relevant to the credibility of a prosecution witness (*Ragg v Magistrates Court of Victoria* (2008) 18 VR 300). This typically includes benefits provided to the witness, including immunities and undertakings offered as incentives for the witness's evidence (see, e.g. (CDPP, 2017, p. 6 [18]). Generally, indemnities provide witnesses with protection from prosecution for the offences about which they testify, whereas undertakings protect a witness from their testimony, or their statements being used against them (but see *Director of Public Prosecutions Act 1983* (Cth) s 6D). Indemnities and undertakings are given by the directors of the prosecution bodies (e.g. WA; TAS *Director of Public Prosecution Act 1973* (TAS), s 12(1) (eb); DPPSA, 2014, p. 11; *Public Prosecutions Act 1994* (VIC) s 22(1)(ca)-(cb); or by the relevant Attorneys General (ODPPQLD, 2016, p. 46; ODPPNSW, 2021, [11.4]; *Criminal Procedure Act 1986* (NSW) ss 32. As an example of prevalence, over 2022–2023, the Commonwealth Director of Public Prosecutions provided 20 undertakings and 3 indemnities[2] (CDPP, 2023a, p. 79). The Office of Public Prosecutions Victoria reported 13 undertakings provided over the same period but no indemnities (OPP, 2023b, p. 93).

Courts can also grant a certificate to protect an informer witness from the evidence provided under the certificate from being used against them in any criminal proceedings, except for perjury related to their testimony (*Uniform Evidence Acts,* s128). These do not, however, grant immunity from prosecution (*Spence v The Queen* [2016] VSCA 113, [68]–[9]). The NSW prosecution guidelines include considering whether it would be more appropriate for the court to issue a certificate under s 128 *Evidence Act 1995* (NSW) than applying for an indemnity or undertaking ([11.4]).

[2] Note, the *Director of Public Prosecutions Act* 1983 refers to both protection from prosecution and use immunities as undertakings, but the report uses the terminology of indemnities for both.

Prison Informants

The risk of wrongful conviction posed by informer testimony is particularly evident in the context of prison informants. Prison informants are typically prosecution witnesses who give evidence of incriminating statements made by the defendant while they are both incarcerated together. They are sometimes referred to as 'incentivised' informants when they are offered benefits or a reward in exchange for their testimony such as an informer sentencing discount, better prison conditions (e.g. phone calls and contact visits, favourable classifications or transfers, or early parole) (Bagaric et al., 2019; Brown, 1993; Surratt, 2018; Sutterer, 2021).

Prison informants are regarded as inherently unreliable (Elliott, 2003; High, 2021; *Pollitt v The Queen* (1992) 174 CLR 558), and prison informer evidence is recognised as a key contributor to wrongful convictions (Bloom, 2003; High, 2021). Convictions based on prison informant testimony 'cannot be regarded as safe unless the jury were warned against the dangers of convicting on such evidence' (*Pollitt v The Queen* (1992) 174 CLR 558, p.615 per McHugh J). Accordingly, section 165(1)(e) *Evidence Act 1995* (Cth) provides that 'evidence given in a criminal proceeding by a witness who is a prison informer' is evidence of a kind that may be unreliable. Where there is a jury, the judge must, at the request of a party, warn the jury that the evidence may be unreliable, inform the jury of the matters that may cause it to be unreliable, and warn the jury of the need for caution in determining whether to accept the evidence and the weight to be given to it (s 165(2); See also section 31 *Jury Directions Act 2015* (Vic)). A failure by a judge to raise with the jury that the informant received a benefit as the result of an undertaking to give evidence will not necessarily result in a miscarriage of justice. There is no requirement to inform the jury that this might cause the evidence to be unreliable under s 165(2)(b) (*R v Stewart* [2001] NSWCCA 260, [147]). However, as McHugh J pointed out in *Pollitt*, there is a real danger that the potentially unreliable evidence of informers will be accepted (*Pollitt v The Queen* (1992) 174 CLR 558., p. 614). There is also the danger that relying on the false statement of a prison informer could initiate a cascade of errors that leads to a wrongful conviction, as in the case of Tim Anderson.

In 1978, a bomb exploded near the Hilton Hotel in Sydney, killing two council workers and a policeman during a meeting of the Commonwealth Heads of Government. The Crown alleged that the bomb was planted by Pederick who was a member of a religious movement, the Ananda Marga.

The bomb aimed to assassinate the Indian prime minister. Tim Anderson was a prominent Ananda Marga member. The police suspected another Ananda Marga member, Tim Anderson, of being involved in the bombing but lacked sufficient evidence to charge him. He was later arrested in 1989 after Raymond Denning, a notorious prisoner, informed NSW Police that Anderson had made incriminating statements to him while they were both incarcerated together in the intervening period (*Anderson v The Queen* (1991) 53 A Crim R 421). In exchange for that information, Denning received indemnities for interstate armed robbery charges, favourable police character evidence for another offence, and charge reductions, amongst other benefits (Brown, 1993, p. 64). Anderson was convicted of three murder counts but subsequently acquitted after the Court of Criminal Appeal found that the trial miscarried because the evidence implicating Anderson had not been properly investigated and this error was exacerbated by an 'inappropriate and unfair attempt' by the crown prosecutor Mark Tedeschi, QC to persuade the jury to draw inferences that were not properly open on the evidence (*Anderson v The Queen* (1991) 53 A Crim R 421, p. 453).

Cross-examining prison informants is often limited because their testimony is difficult to challenge. The incentives received by informants are usually not formalised but rather are based on implicit understandings that favourable testimony will be rewarded. The lack of information makes it difficult for defence counsel to test the reliability of the evidence (Anderson & Morgan, 2021).

Covert Investigative Techniques: Mr Big

The use of deception is a common covert investigative tool for police, such as assuming a false identity to infiltrate a criminal gang (Joh, 2015; *Tofilau v The Queen* (2007) 231 CLR 396, p. 403, Gleeson CJ; *R v Swaffield* (1998) 192 CLR 159, 185-6, Brennan CJ). Australian law, however, distinguishes between the use of deception by police during official questioning and the use of deception by covert police. Police can use lies during police interviews to provoke an admission from a suspect, but any admission or other evidence obtained from the lie may be excluded through the courts' discretion to exclude improperly or illegally obtained evidence. Specifically, section 138(2) of the *UEA* provides that evidence of an admission obtained during or in consequence of questioning is taken to have been obtained improperly if the questioner lied and knew or ought to have known that the lie was likely to elicit an admission.

This limitation, however, will not generally apply to undercover police unless the admissions were elicited by covert police in breach of the suspect's right to silence such as in *R v Swaffield* (1998) 192 CLR 159 ('*Swaffield*') where covert recordings between Swaffield and an undercover police officer were rejected as inadmissible because Swaffield had communicated his desire to remain silent during an earlier formal police interview in relation to the same offences. Mr. Big confessions however are treated differently. The 'Mr Big' scenario technique is a covert investigative method which has been used in Australia for over 25 years. The aim of the technique is to elicit a confession from a suspect when the police lack sufficient evidence to charge (Dufraimont, 2015, p. 477). The police create a fake criminal gang headed by a 'Mr Big' and slowly involve the suspect in the fictional criminal activities of the gang through a series of detailed scenarios (Connors et al., 2017; Murphy & Anderson, 2016; Phelan, 2019). The suspect is told that Mr. Big can make problems 'go away' and if the suspect wants to join the gang, they must tell Mr. Big about their involvement in the crime under investigation (*Tofilau v The Queen* (2007) 231 CLR 396, p. 410).

The tactic was first developed in Canada and introduced by Victoria Police in the late 1990s, initially to help further cold case investigations (*R v Favata* [2004] VSC 7). As Mr. Big operations rely heavily on inducements and pressure offered to suspects, there are concerns that suspects may be induced into making false confessions through Mr. Big Operations (Murphy & Anderson, 2016; Smith et al., 2010). Establishing that a Mr. Big confession is false in Australia is difficult, however, because a key protection does not apply to confessions elicited in this way. The circumstances in which Australian Mr. Big Operations are typically conducted also tend not to attract the discretionary powers of the court to exclude or limit the use of evidence as the criminal activities are simulated and Mr. Big targets are told they are free to walk away (Ruyters & Bartle, 2024).

Under Section 85 of the *Uniform Evidence Acts*, admissions as the result of the act of a person the accused believes to be capable of influencing decisions about prosecuting the accused are not admissible unless it is unlikely that the truth of the admission was adversely affected. The circumstances that the court can look at include any relevant condition or characteristic of the person making the admission, such as the person's mental or intellectual disability, the nature of the questioning, or any inducements made to the person questioned (s85(3)). The courts, however, have been clear in interpreting that this sub-section does not apply to inducements held out by covert police (*R v Kilincer (No. 2)* [2021] NSWSC 829 ([194] (Johnson J)) and *R v Rumsby* [2023] NSWSC 229, ([188] (Hulme JA)).

Confessions from Mr. Big Operations have been admitted into evidence in all reported cases to date (Ruyters & Bartle, 2024, p. 11), and there has not been an established wrongful conviction case resulting from a Mr. Operation in Australia. Confessions are considered potentially unreliable evidence (e.g. *Evidence Act* 1995 (NSW) s 165(1)(a)). Judges, when requested, are generally required to caution juries about deciding to accept this kind of evidence (see, e.g. *Evidence Act* 1995 (Cth), s 165(2)–(3)) and may suggest the jury look for supporting evidence such as non-public information in a suspect's confession. Our analysis of 22 reported Mr. Big cases in Australia found inconsistencies in the supporting evidence relied on in three cases and in the treatment of the inconsistencies by the courts (Ruyters & Bartle, 2024). The two judges in jury trials considered that the discrepancies could be explained (*R v Weaven (No 1)* [2011] VSC 442; *R v Kilincer (No. 2)* [2021] NSWSC 829), whereas Johnson J in *R v Simmons* (No. 5) [2015] NSWSC 333 [482], a judge-only trial, accepted the possibility that the defendant had lied to 'big-note' himself.

Critics remain concerned that these operations erode fundamental rights, such as the right to remain silent and the right to legal representation, both of which are denied to Mr. Big targets (Glazebrook, 2015; Iftene & Kinnear, 2020). In the landmark case *R v Hart* (2014) 2 SCR 544, the Canadian Supreme Court highlighted the potential for Mr. Big operations to become coercive and exploit suspects' vulnerabilities (*Hart,* 2014, [117]; see also *Tofilau* 2007, p. 444, Kirby J). A review of experimental and field data by Otgaar et al. (2021) has also found a relationship between higher levels of suggestibility and compliance in suspects of Mr. Big operations and an increased susceptibility to making false confessions.

There is no independent oversight of Australian Mr. Big operations. The inherent lack of transparency and reliance on deception in this methodology raises concerns about the potential for fabricated or coerced confessions, increasing the risk of wrongful convictions (Ruyters & Bartle, 2024).

Scientific Content Analysis

Similarly, there is minimal transparency over police use of junk science credibility assessment techniques in their investigations. The investigative interview is a crucial aspect of any police investigation, focusing on assessing the credibility of suspects and witnesses and detecting deception (Gudjonsson & Pearse, 2011), and various credibility assessment tools have been developed to aid interviewers in this task (Nicklaus & Stein, 2020; Vrij, 2008), including Scientific Content Analysis (SCAN), also known as statement analysis (Bogaard et al., 2016; Heydon, 2008; Vrij, 2008). SCAN was created by Avinoam Sapir, a former Israeli polygraph examiner, based on the premise that liars and truth-tellers use different languages during interviews (Sapir, 1987). The SCAN process is aimed at eliciting a clear statement for thorough analysis for the purpose of detecting signs of deception (Goormans et al., 2022). The interviewee is asked to write down everything about a specific event without any guidance. The written statement is then analysed using SCAN criteria to identify 'highlights' or 'hotspots' that may indicate deception. These criteria used can vary between investigators (Oberlader et al., 2021). A comprehensive list of known criteria, adapted from (Bockstaele, 2019) and cited in Goormans et al. (2022), is provided in Table 11.1. These 'hotspots' are explored in subsequent interviews to detect deception.

SCAN has been criticised for its lack of standardisation and insufficient evidence supporting its accuracy in detecting deception (Bogaard et al., 2014b; Driscoll, 1994; Nahari et al., 2012; Porter & Yuille, 1996). Consequently, it is generally considered unreliable as an investigative tool (Bogaard et al., 2014a; Kang & Lee, 2014; Kleinberg et al., 2019; Smith

Table 11.1 List of SCAN criteria (provided in Bockstaele, 2019)

1. Change in language use	9. Structure of the statement
2. Lack of memory of the event	10. Not answering the question
3. Unnecessary links	11. Evasive answers
4. Out-of-sequence information	12. Change in verb tense
5. The place of emotions within the statement	13. Lack of social introduction
6. Sensory perceptions	14. Missing information (text bridges)
7. Spontaneous denials/corrections	15. Details within the statement
8. Inappropriate use of pronouns	16. Time

& Willis, 2001). The use of SCAN may also increase the risk of contextual or expectancy bias, leading to 'tunnel vision' in investigations, which is a significant factor in wrongful convictions (Komel et al., 2020; Risinger et al., 2002; Vanderhallen et al., 2016). Despite these concerns, police continue to use SCAN in their investigations (Bogaard et al., 2016).

SCAN has been used by Australian policing agencies from at least the late 1990s. Recently, it was revealed in a Channel 4 documentary 'Murder in The Outback' covering the murder of the 28-year-old British tourist Peter Falconio that the police initially became suspicious of the accounts of Falconio's partner, Joanne Lees, based on an erroneous SCAN analysis (Meyrick & Arwel-Lewis, 2020). On the night of 14 July 2001 Falconio and Lees were driving on an isolated road when a man driving a four-wheel-drive vehicle flagged them down, indicating that something was wrong with their camper van. When Falconio stopped the vehicle and got out to investigate, the man—later identified as Bradley John Murdoch—ambushed them. According to Lees, Murdoch shot Falconio and then attempted to abduct her. Lees was tied up with cable ties, but she managed to escape and hide in the bushes for several hours, eventually flagging down a passing truck for help (*The Queen v Murdoch* [2005] NTSC 77 [4]–[9]). The documentary found that a SCAN expert was utilised by NT Police to analyse the initial interview with Lees. The SCAN report suggested that Lees was deceptive, leading to initial suspicion by investigators regarding the accuracy of Lees' account. This assessment was later admitted to be inaccurate by the expert in his interview with documentarians (Singh, 2020).

Polygraphs

The polygraph is another "junk science" credibility assessment technique used by police. A polygraph instrument measures a person's physiological changes in their response to questions. The US National Research Council's 2003 review on polygraphs and lie detection was critical of the poor quality and inherent biases in observational testing of polygraphs in the field but did concede a median accuracy index "well above chance" (National Research Council, 2003, p. 4).

Polygraphs have featured in very few Australian cases, but courts have expressed concern about the reliability of lie detection and polygraph testing as a recognised field of expertise. Courts in *Mallard v The Queen* "Mallard" (2003) 28 WAR 1 and in *R v Murray* "Murray" (1981) 7 A

Crim R 48 considered the admissibility of evidence of polygraph tests (see also Edelman, 2005; Freckelton, 2004). In *Mallard's* case, the Court of Appeal heard evidence from a polygraph examiner who had tested Mallard and expert evidence on the effectiveness of polygraph examinations. The Court of Criminal Appeal held (2003, p. 73):

> In substance, we are not satisfied on the evidence that polygraphic examination (specifically CQT) has been accepted to any appreciable extent as scientifically valid and reliable, by members of the psychological and psychophysiological community … as to constitute part of a body of knowledge or experience which is sufficiently recognised to be accepted as a reliable body of knowledge or experience. Nor has it been shown to have a sufficient scientific basis to render results arrived at by the application of polygraphic technique part of a field of knowledge which is a proper subject of expert evidence.

Murray had sought to adduce evidence of a polygraph examination he had undertaken to support his denials that he had fired shots at police officers. Sinclair DCJ held that evidence of the results of a polygraph examination was inadmissible for several reasons, including that the scientific premise on which the assessment was based had not been established in Australia (*Murray,* 1981, p. 49). Sinclair DCJ concluded that this 'evangelical sideline' had no place 'in a criminal trial in New South Wales (1981, p. 50). Unique in Australia, section 6 of the *Lie Detectors Act* 1983 (NSW) also explicitly provides that outputs of polygraph examinations are not admissible as evidence.

Use of Polygraph Examinations as an Investigative Tool

Polygraph tests might not be admissible as evidence because of concerns of its reliability and validity, but other than New South Wales, the technique is still available for police to use as an investigative tool (*R v Trochym* [2007] 1 SCR 239 [62]). Police use lie detection tests to eliminate or confirm suspects, identify whether suspects have exaggerated or omitted information, place pressure on suspects, obtain admissions, and as indicators of guilt (McMahon, 2003, pp. 29, 46). They are generally used as a last resort when other investigative avenues have failed (McMahon, 2003, p. 41). The testing is an "event-specific" investigation, such as after a crime (National Research Council, 2003, p. 1). There is little available information about the current use of polygraphs by Australian police; however, there is evidence it was in use in Queensland, Victoria, and Western Australia in the early 2000s (McMahon, 2003, pp. 26, 40, 41; *R v Clarke* [2004] VSC 11 [15]). The use of polygraphs in police investigations, however, is prohibited in New South Wales. Section 5 of the *Lie Detectors Act 1983* (NSW) makes it an offence to use a polygraph or its output for any prohibited purpose. The definition of "prohibited purpose" in section 4 includes any purpose connected with establishing whether a person is guilty of an offence.

Legislation

Criminal Procedure Act 1986 (NSW)
Director of Public Prosecutions Act 1986 (NSW)
Director of Public Prosecutions Act 1983 (Cth)
Director of Public Prosecution Act 1973 (TAS)
Evidence Act 1995 (NSW)
Human Source Management Act 2023 (Vic)
Lie Detectors Act 1983 (NSW)
Uniform Evidence Acts

Cases

AB v CD & EF. (2017). *VSCA*, 338.
AB v CD; EF v CD. (2018). *HCA*, 58.
Alister v The Queen (1984) 154 CLR 404
Anderson v The Queen (1991) 53 A Crim R 421
Carter v The Managing Partner, Northmore Hale Davy and Leake and Others (1995) 183 CLR 121
Cvetanovski v The Queen [2020] VSCA 272
Farrell v The Queen (1998) 194 CLR 286
Jarvie v Magistrates' Court of Victoria at Brunswick [1995] 1 VR 84
Kant v DPP (1994) 73 A Crim R 481
Mallard v The Queen (2003) 28 WAR 1
Marks v Beyfus (1890) LR 25 QBD 494
Orman v The Queen [2019] VSCA 163
Pollitt v The Queen (1992) 174 CLR 55
R v Clarke [2004] VSC 11
R v David (1986) 23 A Crim R 159
R v Hart (2014) 2 SCR 544

R v Jarrett (1994) 73 A Crim R
R v Kilincer (No. 2) [2021] NSWSC 829
R v Murray (1981) 7 A Crim R 48
R v Rumsby [2023] NSWSC 229
R v Simmons (No. 5) [2015] NSWSC 333
R v Stewart [2001] NSWCCA 260
R v Swaffield (1998) 192 CLR 159
R v Trochym [2007] 1 SCR 239
R v Weaven (No 1) [2011] VSC 442
Ragg v Magistrates Court of Victoria (2008) 18 VR 300
Royal Women's Hospital v Medical Practitioners Board (2006) 15 VR 22
Spence v The Queen. (2016). *VSCA*, 113.
Tofilau v The Queen (2007) 231 CLR 396

References

Anderson, P., & Morgan, C. L. (2021). Snitched on or stitched up? A review of the law in New Zealand in relation to jailhouse informant evidence - part 1. *New Zealand Law Journal*, 119–123.

Bagaric, M., Xynas, L., & McCord, D. (2019). Should we flip on flippers: A rational approach to providing penalty reductions to criminal informers. *Tennessee Law Review, 87*, 121.

Bloom, R. M. (2003). Jailhouse informants. *Criminal Justice, 18*, 20.

Bockstaele, M. (2019). SCAN versus experimenteel wetenschappelijk onderzoek. *Panopticon, 40*(2), 120.

Bogaard, G., Meijer, E. H., Vrij, A., Broers, N. J., & Merckelbach, H. (2014a). Contextual bias in verbal credibility assessment: Criteria-based content analysis, reality monitoring and scientific content analysis. *Applied Cognitive Psychology, 28*(1), 79–90.

Bogaard, G., Meijer, E. H., Vrij, A., Broers, N. J., & Merckelbach, H. (2014b). SCAN is largely driven by 12 criteria: Results from sexual abuse statements. *Psychology, Crime & Law, 20*(5), 430–449.

Bogaard, G., Meijer, E. H., Vrij, A., & Merckelbach, H. (2016). Scientific content analysis (SCAN) cannot distinguish between truthful and fabricated accounts of a negative event. *Frontiers in Psychology, 7*, 243. https://doi.org/10.3389/fpsyg.2016.00243

Brown, D. (1993). Notes on the culture of prison informing. *Current Issues in Criminal Justice, 5*(1), 54–71.

Commonwealth Director of Public Prosecutions. (2017). *Statement on disclosure.* Retrieved 07/11/2024 from

Connors, C. J., Archibald, N., Smith, S. M., & Patry, M. W. (2017). Shocking the conscience: Public responses to police use of the "Mr. Big" technique. *Journal of Forensic Psychology Research and Practice, 17*(1), 25–37.

Driscoll, L. N. (1994). A validity assessment of written statements from suspects in criminal investigations using the SCAN technique. *Police Studies: International Review of Police Development, 17*, 77.

Dufraimont, L. (2015). *Hart and Mack: New restraints on Mr. Big and a new approach to unreliable prosecution evidence.* The Supreme Court Law Review: Osgoode's Annual Constitutional Cases Conference.

Edelman, J. (2005). The admissibility of polygraph (Lie Detector) examinations. *Criminal Law Journal, 29*(1), 21–36.

Elliott, C. B. (2003). Life's uncertainties: How to deal with cooperating witnesses and jailhouse snitches. *CAPS's Defence Journal, 16*, 1.

Freckelton, I. (2004). The closing of the coffin on forensic polygraph evidence for Australia: Mallard v The Queen [2003] WASCA 296. *Psychiatry, Psychology and Law, 11*(2), 359–366.

Garrett, B. L. (2011). *Convicting the innocent: Where criminal prosecutions go wrong.* Harvard University Press. https://doi.org/10.4159/harvard.9780674060982

Garrett, B. L. (2015). *Convicting the innocent redux. Wrongful convictions and the DNA revolution: Twenty-five years of freeing the innocent* (Cambridge University Press, Forthcoming), Duke Law School Public Law & Legal Theory Series.

Glazebrook, S. (2015). *Mr Big Operations: Innovative Investigative Technique or Threat to Justice? Speech given by the Honourable Justice Dame Susan Glazebrook at the Judicial Colloquium.* Retrieved September

Goormans, I., Mergaerts, L., & Vandeviver, C. (2022). *SCANning for truth. Scholars' and practitioners' perceptions on the use (fulness) of scientific content analysis in detecting deception during police interviews* (pp. 1–23). Psychology, Crime & Law.

Gould, J., Carrano, J., Leo, R. A., & Hail-Jares, K. (2013). Predicting erroneous convictions. *Iowa Law Review, 99*, 471.

Gudjonsson, G. H., & Pearse, J. (2011). Suspect interviews and false confessions. *Current Directions in Psychological Science, 20*(1), 33–37.

Heydon, G. (2008). *Are police organisations suspending their disbelief in Scientific Content Analysis (SCAN)?, XXXXX*, 8.

High, A. (2021). The exclusion of prison informant evidence for unreliability in New Zealand. *The International Journal of Evidence & Proof, 25*(3), 217–238.

Iftene, A., & Kinnear, V. L. (2020). Mr. Big and the new common law confessions rule: Five years in review. *Man. LJ, 43*, 295.

Integrity, O. o. P. (2007a). *Ceja task force drug related corruption third and final report.* V. Government.

Integrity, O. o. P. (2007b). *Past patterns-future directions: Victoria Police and the problem of corruption and serious misconduct.* V. g. printer. https://vgls.sdp.sirsidynix.net.au/client/search/asset/1148093

Joh, E. (2015). Bait, mask, and ruse: Technology and police deception. *Harvard Law Review, 128*(6), 246–252.

Kang, S.-M., & Lee, H. (2014). Detecting deception by analyzing written statements in Korean. *Linguistic Evidence in Security, Law and Intelligence, 2*(2).

Kleinberg, B., Arntz, A., & Verschuere, B. (2019). Being accurate about accuracy in verbal deception detection. *PLoS One, 14*(8), e0220228.

Komel, M., Šterk, K., Župan Galunić, A., & Savić, G. (2020). SCAN revisited through linguistic psychoanalysis. *Kriminalistička teorija i praksa, 7*(1/2020.), 7–30.

Lusty, D. (2002). Anonymous accusers: An historical & comparative analysis of secret witnesses in criminal trials. *The Sydney Law Review, 24*(3), 361–426.

Mares, H. (2002). Balancing public interest and a fair trial in police informer privilege: A critical Australian perspective. *The International Journal of Evidence & Proof, 6*(2), 94–124.

McMahon, M. (2003). Polygraph testing for deception in Australia: Effective aid to crime investigation and adjudication? *Journal of Law and Medicine, 11*(1), 24–47.

McMurdo, M. A. (2020). Royal Commission into the Management of Police Informants, *Final Report*. V. Government. rcmpi.vic.gov.au/final-report

Meyrick, S., & Arwel-Lewis, B. (2020). *Murder in the outback*. In.

Murphy, B., & Anderson, J. (2016). Confessions to Mr Big: A new rule of evidence? *The International Journal of Evidence & Proof, 20*(1), 29–48.

Nahari, G., Vrij, A., & Fisher, R. P. (2012). Does the truth come out in the writing? Scan as a lie detection tool. *Law and Human Behavior, 36*(1), 68.

National Research Council. (2003). *The polygraph and lie detection*. The National Academic Press, Committee to Review the Scientific Evidence on the Polygraph, Division of Behavioral and Social Science and Education.

Nicklaus, M., & Stein, D. (2020). The role of linguistics in veracity evaluation. *JLL, 9*, 23.

Oberlader, V. A., Quinten, L., Banse, R., Volbert, R., Schmidt, A. F., & Schönbrodt, F. D. (2021). Validity of content-based techniques for credibility assessment—How telling is an extended meta-analysis taking research bias into account? *Applied Cognitive Psychology, 35*(2), 393–410.

Office of Director of Public Prosecutions New South Wales. (2021). *Prosecution Guidelines*. In. New South Wales: Office of Director of Public Prosecutions New South Wales.

Office of Public Prosecutions Victoria. (2022). *Protocol for engagement and resolution of complex issues arising from disclosure obligations and public interest immunity claims*. In: Office of Public Prosecutions Victoria.

Otgaar, H., Schell-Leugers, J. M., Howe, M. L., Vilar, A. D. L. F., Houben, S. T., & Merckelbach, H. (2021). The link between suggestibility, compliance, and false confessions: A review using experimental and field studies. *Applied Cognitive Psychology, 35*(2), 445–455.

Phelan, N. (2019). Importing a Canadian creation: A comparative analysis of evidentiary rules governing the admissibility of confessions to Mr. *Big. Man. LJ, 42*, 385.

Police, V. (1991). *Exhibit RC0008 Annexure 30 Force Circular Memo No. 91-9, 17 December 1991.* In. Melbourne: Royal Commission into the Management of Police Informants.

Porter, S., & Yuille, J. C. (1996). The language of deceit: An investigation of the verbal clues to deception in the interrogation context. *Law and Human Behavior, 20*(4), 443–458.

Prosecutions, C. D. o. P. (2023a). *Commonwealth Director of Public Prosecutions (CDPP) Annual Report 2022-2023.* C. o. Australia. https://www.cdpp.gov.au/sites/default/files/CDPP%202022-23%20Annual%20report.pdf

Prosecutions, O. o. P. (2023b). *Office of Public Prosecutions Victoria Annual Report 2022/2023.* O. o. P. Prosecutions. https://www.opp.vic.gov.au/wp-content/uploads/2024/02/OPP-Annual-Report-2022-23-final.pdf

Risinger, D. M., Saks, M. J., Thompson, W. C., & Rosenthal, R. (2002). The Daubert/Kumho implications of observer effects in forensic science: Hidden problems of expectation and suggestion. *California Law Review, 90*, 1.

Ruyters, M., & Bartle, J. (2024). Who's watching Mr Big? Scenario operations and induced confessions. *Current Issues in Criminal Justice, 1–16*, 36.

Sapir, A. (1987). *The LSI course on scientific content analysis (SCAN).* Laboratory for Scientific Interrogation.

Singh, A. (2020, 03/06/2020). Peter Falconio and Joanne lees mystery: New documentary raises questions about outback case. *The Telegraph.* https://www.telegraph.co.uk/news/2020/06/03/peter-falconio-joanne-lees-mystery-new-documentary-raises-questions/

Smith, N., & Willis, C. F. (2001). *Reading between the lines: An evaluation of the scientific content analysis technique (SCAN)* (Vol. 135). Citeseer.

Smith, S. M., Stinson, V., & Patry, M. W. (2010). High-risk interrogation: Using the "Mr. Big technique" to elicit confessions. *Law and Human Behavior, 34*(1), 39–40.

Surratt, M. (2018). Incentivized informants, Brady, Ruiz, and wrongful imprisonment: Requiring pre-plea disclosure of material exculpatory evidence. *Washington Law Review, 93*, 523.

Sutterer, J. (2021). Snitches cause stitches: The need for legislative reform on jailhouse informant testimony laws. *Journal of Legislation, 48*, 337.

Vanderhallen, M., Jaspaert, E., & Vervaeke, G. (2016). SCAN as an investigative tool. *Police Practice and Research, 17*(3), 279–293.

Vrij, A. (2008). *Detecting lies and deceit: Pitfalls and opportunities.* Wiley.

CHAPTER 12

Conclusion

Abstract This chapter concludes with the identification of interconnected risks contributing to wrongful convictions in the Australian context that can be indicators for others working internationally. These risks include chronic underfunding of legal aid, systemic racial disadvantages, language and linguistic barriers, and a persistent police culture of misconduct. We argue that these deeply ingrained issues within Australia's cultural, political, and social structures resist reform and disproportionately affect vulnerable populations, particularly Indigenous Australians. Furthermore, we highlight that inadequate resources hinder both defence and prosecution, potentially leading to errors and breaches in due process. Finally, we emphasise the need for increased support and funding to address these pre-conviction risks, as the very risks causing wrongful convictions also impede their rectification. Ultimately, without proactive intervention, miscarriages of justice will continue to plague the Australian legal system.

Keywords Wrongful conviction • Risk • Causal factors • Systemic issues • Innocence

The aim of our book is to stimulate research and understanding of the many influences, causes, and factors that contribute to wrongful convictions in Australia. Most of the risks we identify intersect in ways that

M. Ruyters et al., *Innocence Unveiled*,
https://doi.org/10.1007/978-3-031-91343-3_12

devastate innocent accused and will continue to do so because they appear cemented in cultural, political, and social dynamics and structures that resist reform. We suggest there are four critical intersecting risks for wrongful conviction in Australia which we hope will stimulate debate and research: longstanding legal assistance and legal funding crisis; language and linguistic disadvantage; systemic racial disadvantage; and a seemingly unbreakable police culture of misconduct. We also point out that managerialist appeal options have a significant role in perpetuating wrongful convictions.

Chronic underfunding in the legal assistance sector exacerbates the risk of wrongful convictions, preventing defence lawyers from adequately preparing cases and securing independent evidence, and reducing defence strategies to attempts to undermine prosecution cases. The situation is aggravated in complex cases involving voluminous evidence such as covert recordings or digital data with legally aided defence lawyers unlikely to be sufficiently funded or resourced to analyse vast volumes of data in prosecution materials. Lawyers often face impossible choices between reviewing all materials without compensation or limiting their review, increasing the likelihood of oversight and procedural errors. A longstanding legal aid crisis has systemic consequences, including delays and increased stress for defence and prosecution lawyers. Mounting caseloads, impacted by COVID-related backlogs and increasingly complex trials, strain both defence and prosecution resources. For prosecution bodies, inadequate funding and overwhelming workloads contribute to the risk of breaches in disclosure duties and procedural errors, further undermining the integrity of trials.

As we have discussed in this book, there is ongoing evidence that police investigations are often influenced by conscious and unconscious biases, particularly racial bias. Racially disproportionate interactions with the police inevitably must end in disproportionate risk of wrongful convictions. Data released in 2024, for instance, revealed that Aboriginal people remain disproportionately represented at each stage of the criminal justice system in New South Wales, comprising more than 30% of the adult prison population while only making up 3.4% of the NSW adult population. This follows reports by the Law Enforcement Commission (LECC) in 2020 and 2023 that NSW police interviewing methods compromised the right to silence for young persons in custody and a vulnerable Aboriginal man (Law Enforcement Conduct Commission, 2023, 2024).

Language, linguistic, and cognitive disadvantages are also deeply entrenched issues in Australia's justice systems, making it impossible for some defendants to participate knowingly in their criminal cases. People with language impairments often struggle with complex legal language, leading to misinterpretations or false admissions. Research shows that many suspects do not understand police cautions, their legislative and common law rights, or the consequences of guilty pleas, which are incentivised by systemic pressures, such as sentencing discounts. Cognitive impairments further exacerbate vulnerabilities in criminal defendants, while among Indigenous Australians, who are 14 times more likely to be imprisoned, disabilities are often underreported. Overall, these factors disproportionately affect Indigenous Australians.

The 'wash, rinse, dry and repeat' cycle of police misconduct in Australia has become normalised and expected. Exposed misconduct followed by institutional chest beating and promises to do better have not changed the inherent risks created by an enduring and deeply flawed police culture. Commissions and inquiries have documented systemic ethical failings in Australian police forces over decades, driven by a results-oriented culture prioritising convictions over justice, endemic resistance to accountability and transparency, and poor oversight and ethical decision-making practices.

Problematically, where the identification of these risks in this book represents an important step into our evolving understanding of wrongful conviction in Australia, our ability to recognise and act on miscarriages of justice remains limited. There is a need for more support to adequately address each of the risks we identify throughout the book. In many cases, this requires funding and support from governments to ensure the faults in our justice system are addressed. Without this support in these areas prior to conviction, significant miscarriages of justice and wrongful conviction will persist. Without pre-emptively addressing these risks, wrongful conviction will continue to be difficult to rectify in Australia because the faults, failures, and risks that lead to error also limit the avenues that we deem legally appropriate to overturn and correct errors in our current system. As a result, the most vulnerable in our communities remain the most likely to be wrongfully convicted but also the most likely to be unable to reclaim their innocence.

References

Law Enforcement Conduct Commission. (2023). *Media Release - Operation Mantus Final Report.* Retrieved 28/11/2024 from https://www.lecc.nsw.gov.au/news/media-release-operation-mantus-final-report

Law Enforcement Conduct Commission. (2024). *Operation Pamir - final report.* https://www.lecc.nsw.gov.au/publications/publications/section-132-report-operation-pamir-october-2024.pdf

Index

M. Ruyters et al., *Innocence Unveiled*,
https://doi.org/10.1007/978-3-031-91343-3

The manufacturer's authorised representative in the EU is Springer Nature Customer Service Centre GmbH, Europaplatz 3, 69115 Heidelberg, Germany. If you have any concerns regarding our products, please contact ProductSafety@springernature.com

Printed and bound by CPI Group (UK) Ltd, Croydon, CR0 4YY
01/10/2026
02225879-0017